Bears

a photographic collection

Kimberli A. Bindschatel

Published by Turning Leaf Productions, LLC.
Traverse City, Michigan

www.KimberliBindschatel.com

ISBN-13: 978-1518807428
ISBN-10: 1518807429

Thank you for purchasing this book and supporting an indie author.

Bears.

Cute and cuddly. Apex predators with the power to kill. Either way, fascinating.

Legends portray bears as ruthless killers of men. Myths abound of their ferocious attacks on defenseless campers, of their blood-thirsty stalking of hikers. In truth, bears are intelligent and resourceful wild animals that deserve our respect. Like all wild animals, they would prefer to avoid us. Elusive and shy, we are lucky to catch a glimpse of a bear in the wild.

Enjoy these glimpses of one of the most majestic animals on Earth.

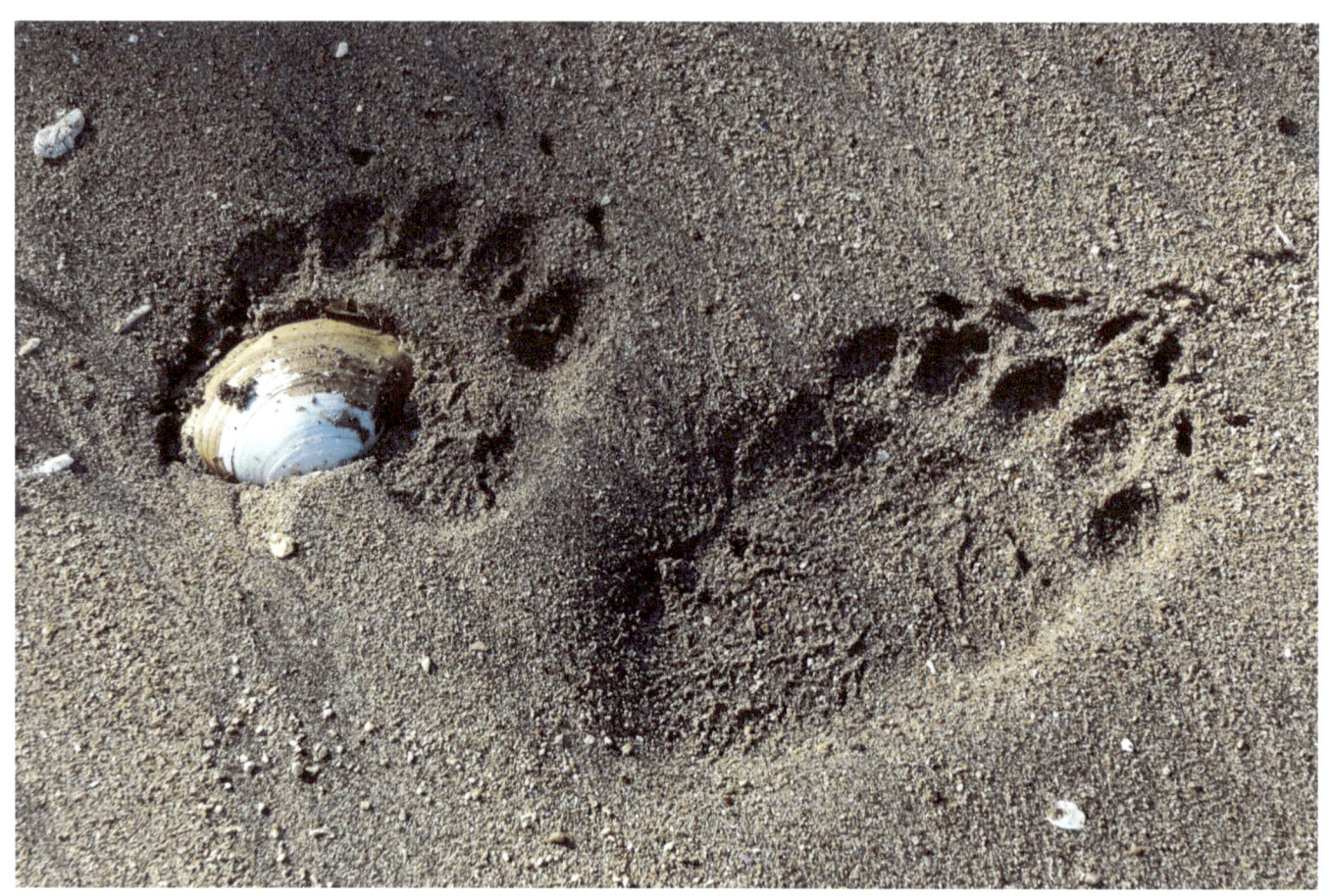

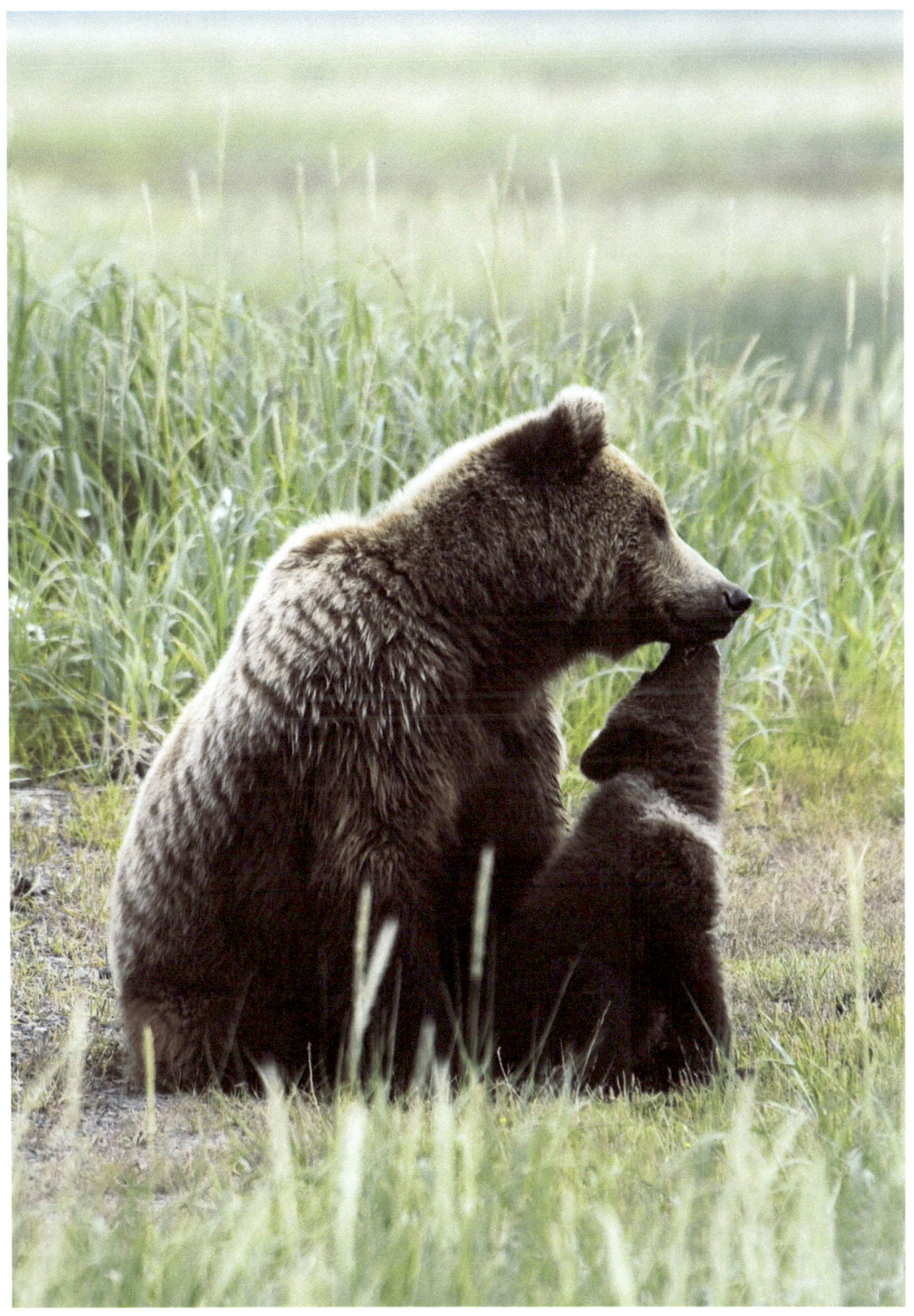

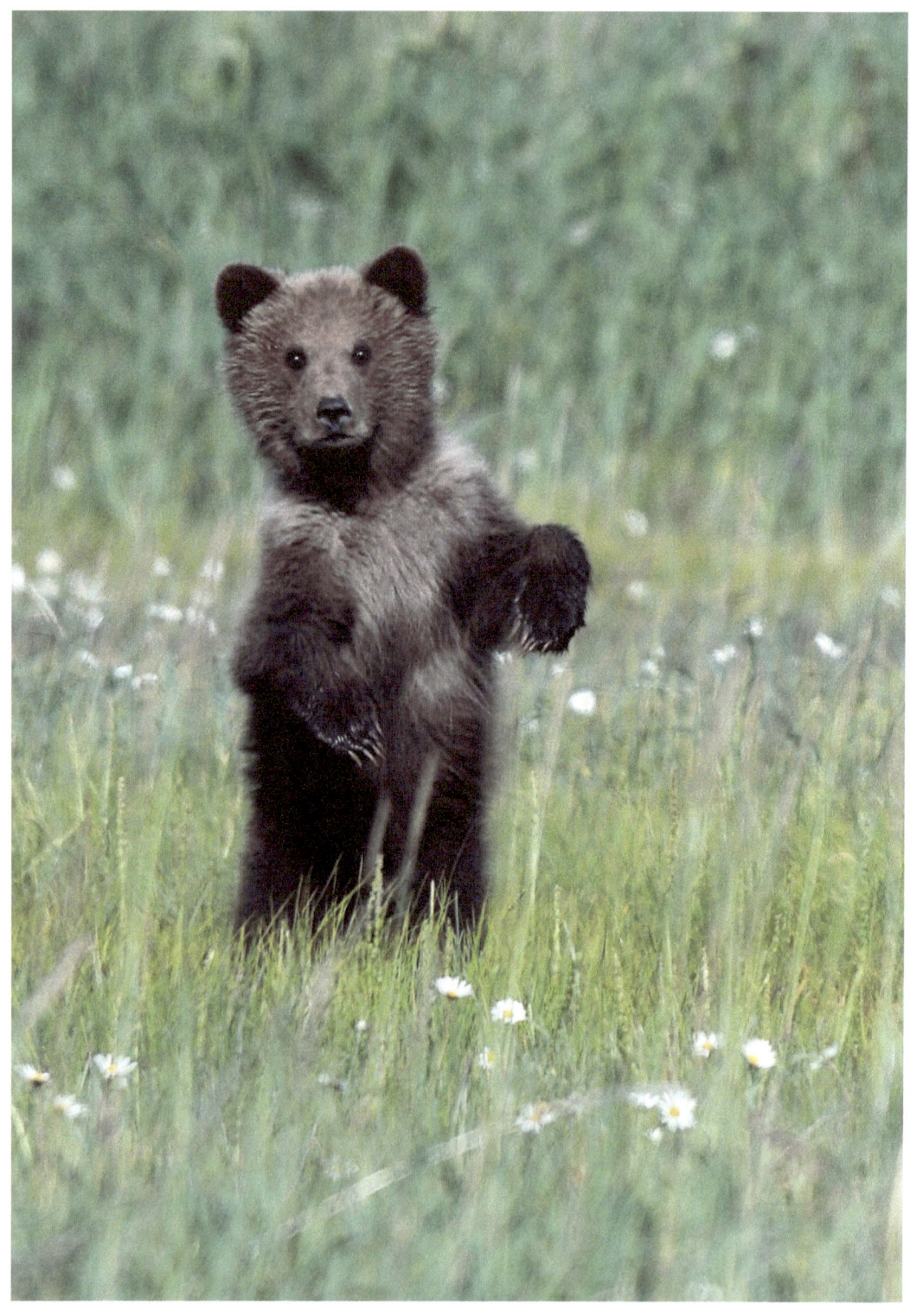

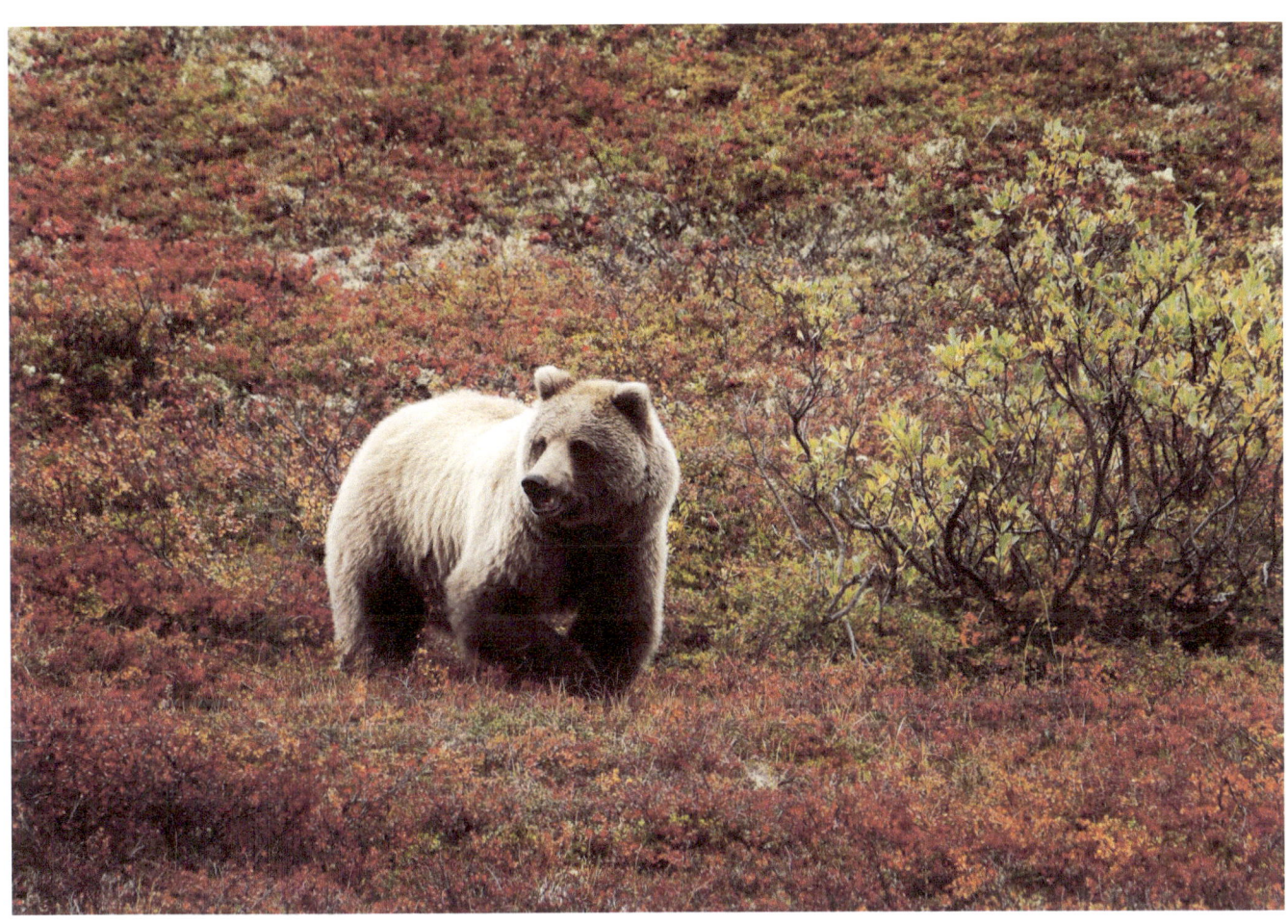

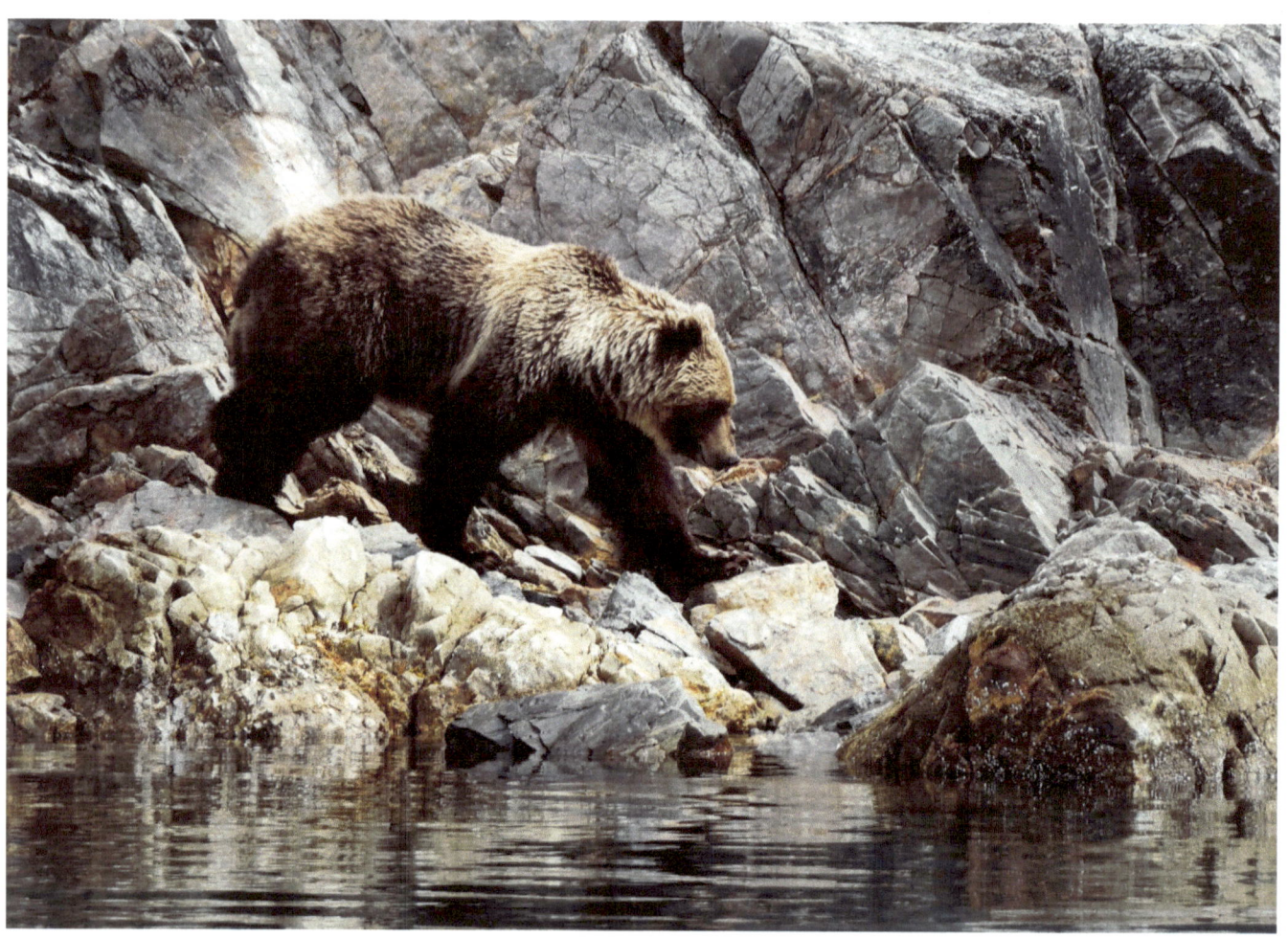

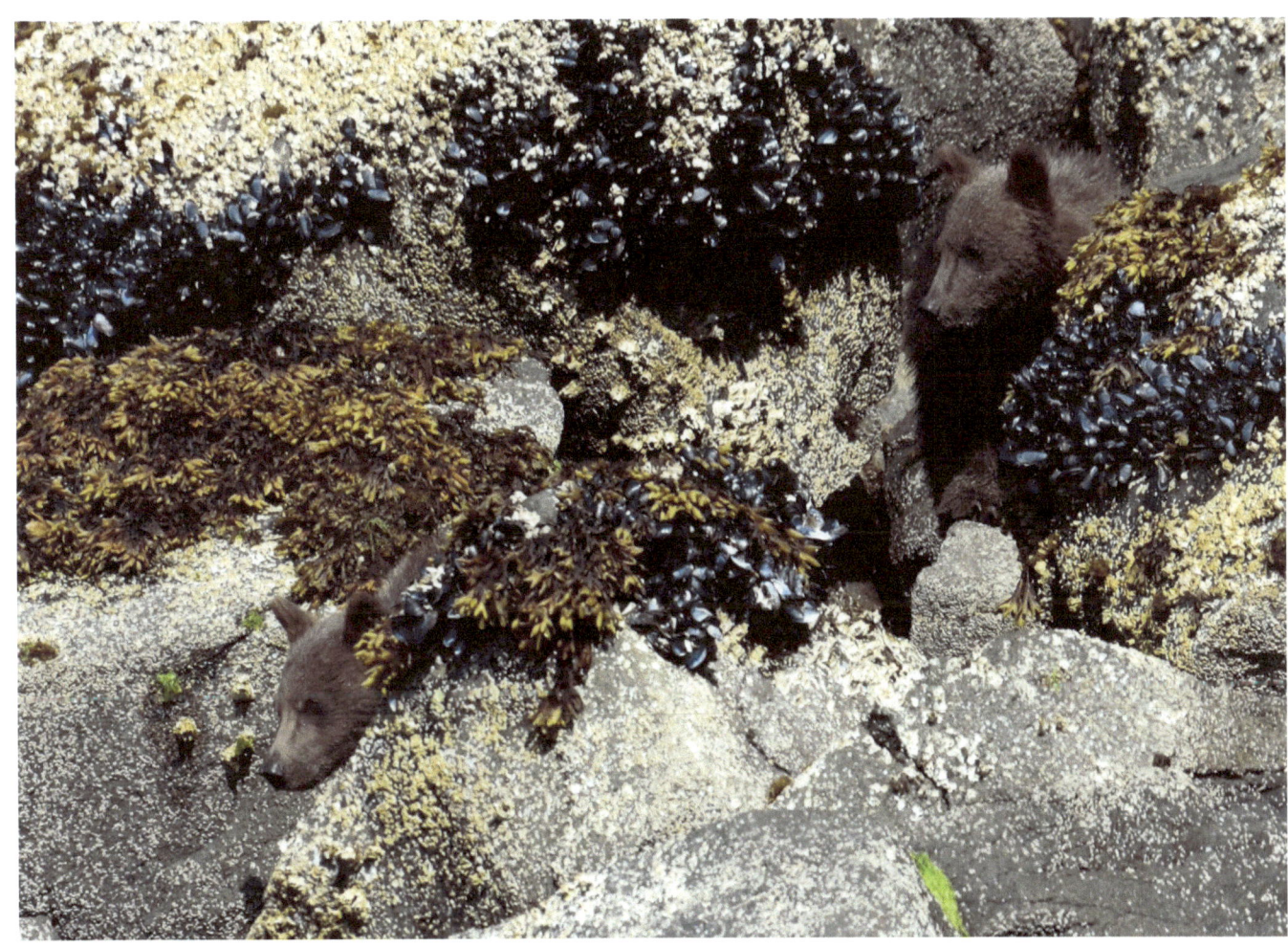

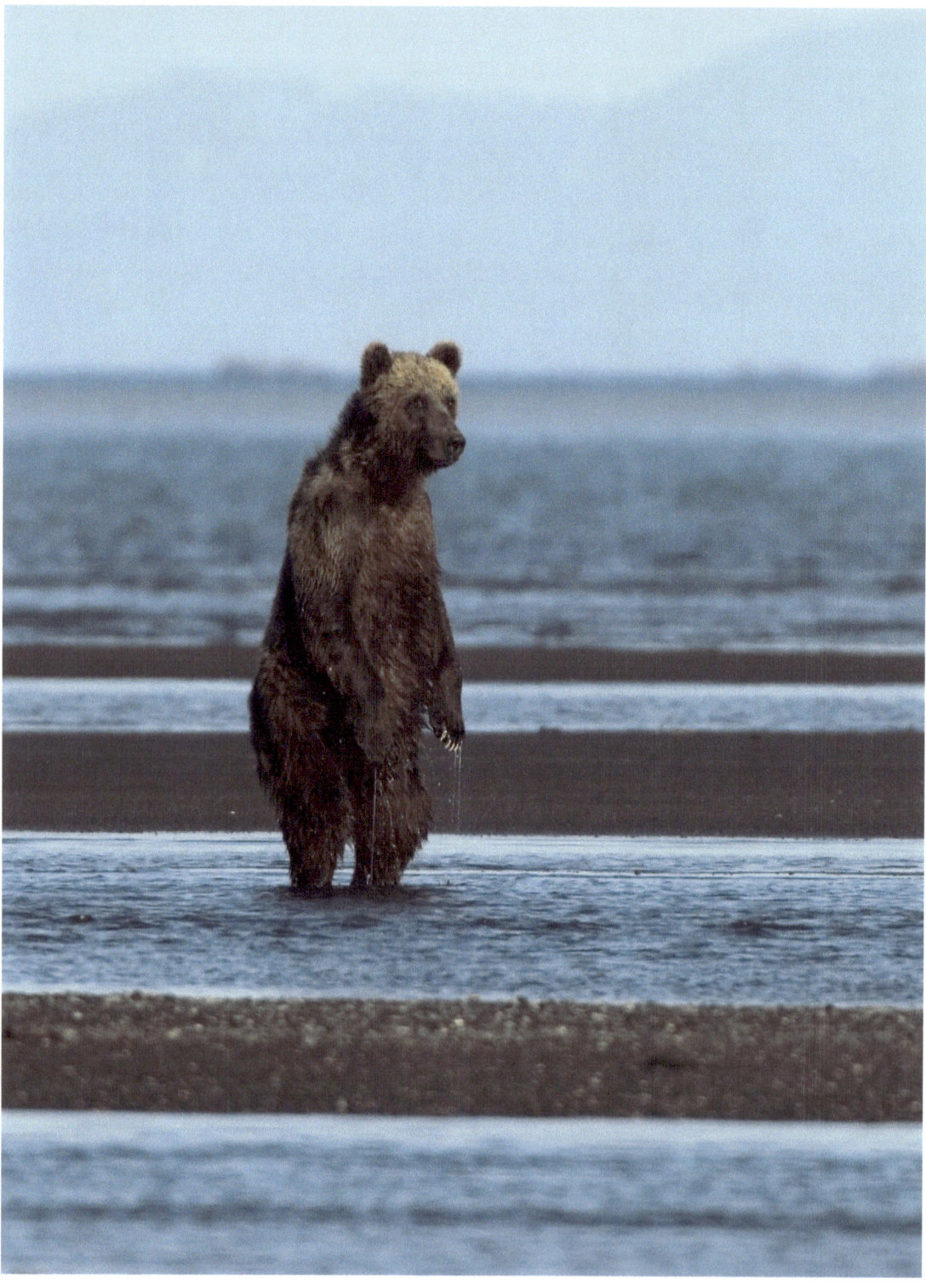

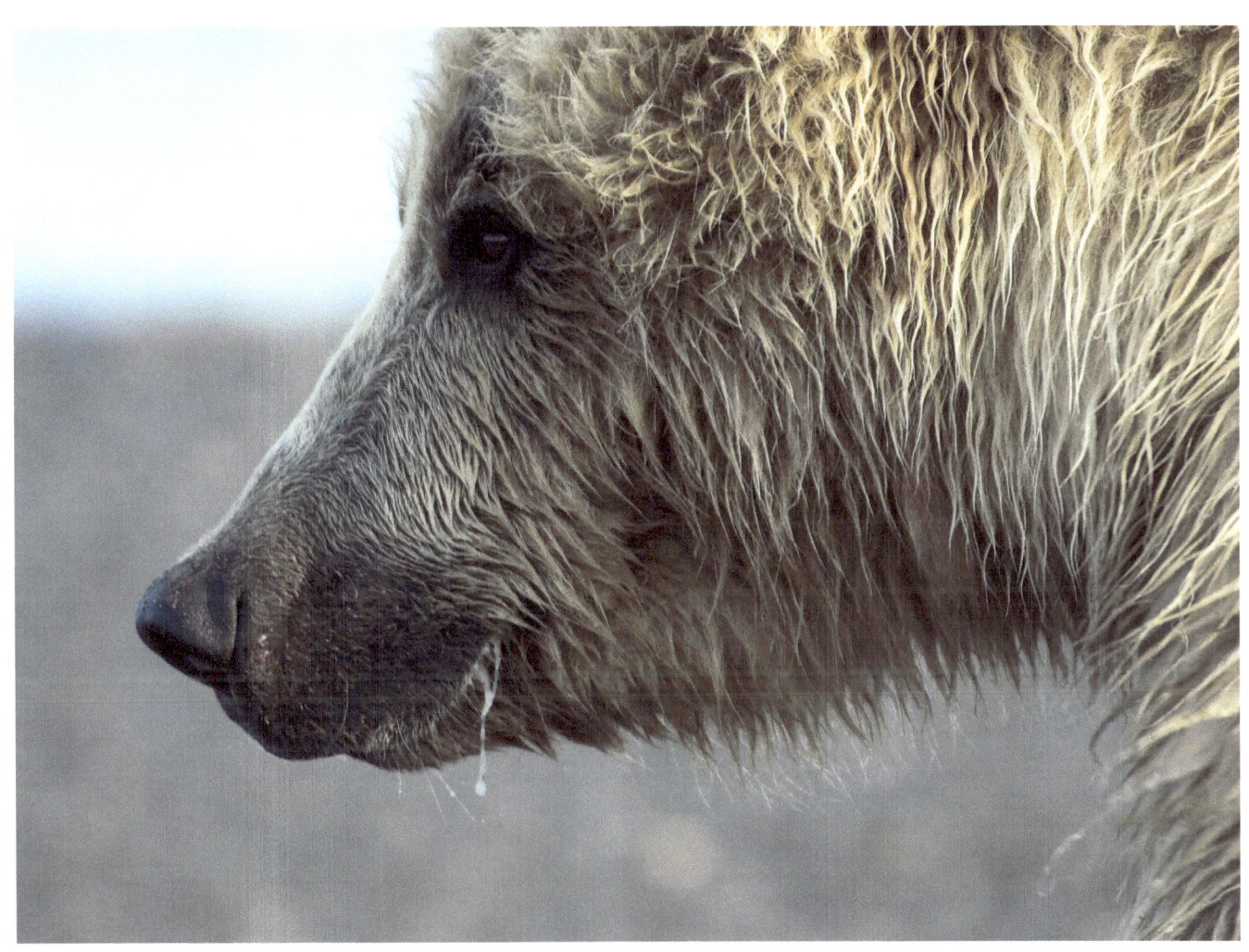

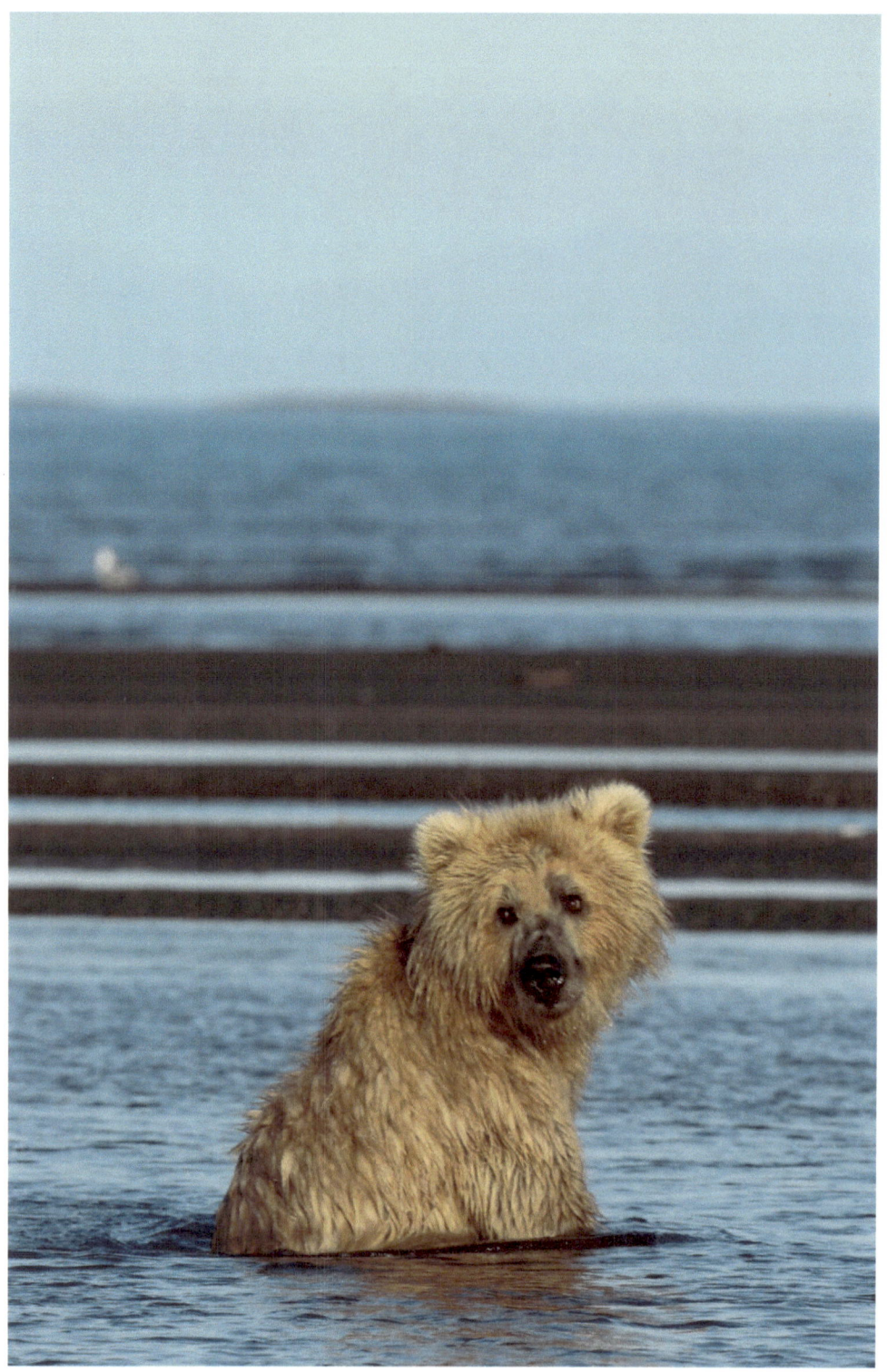

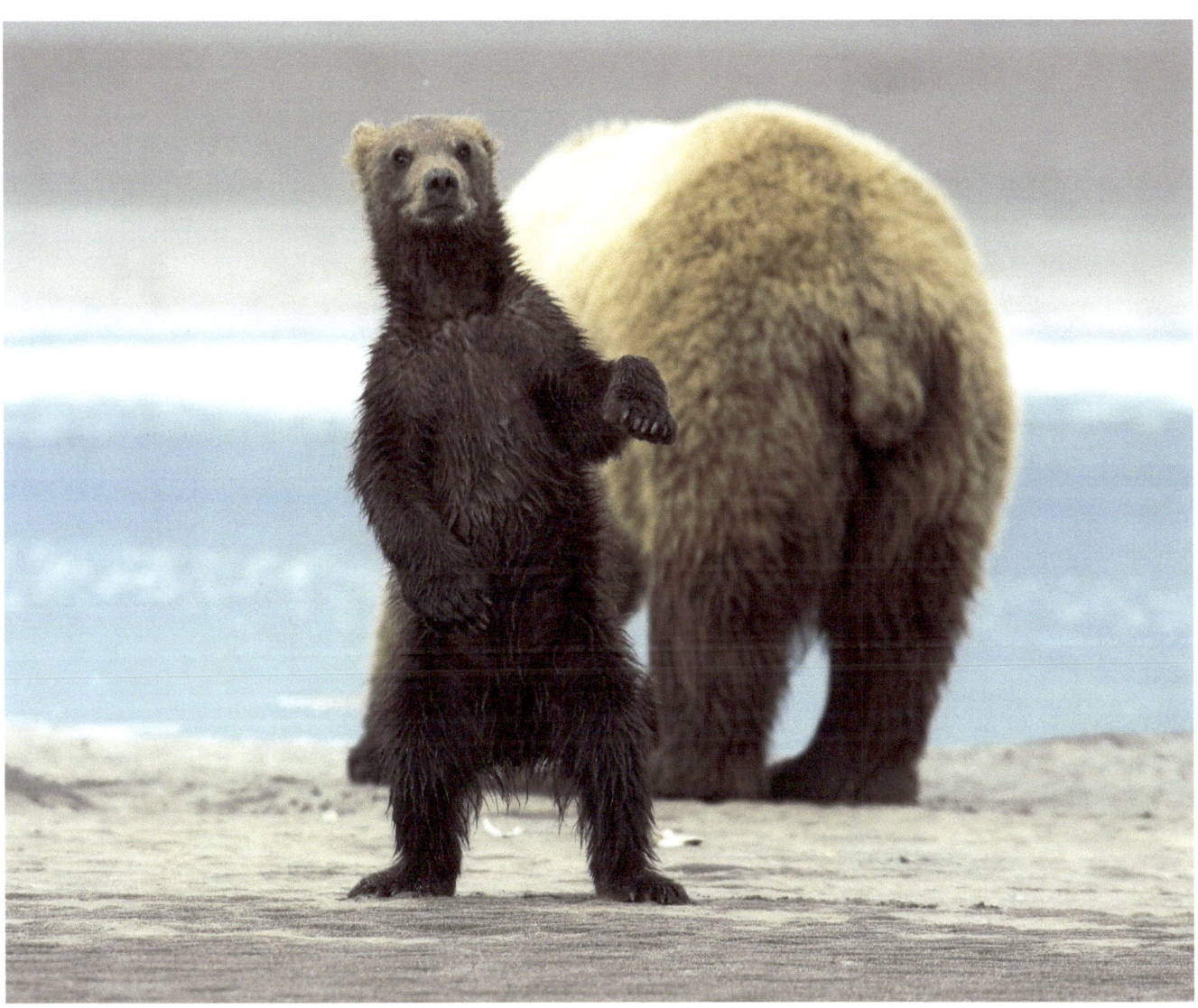

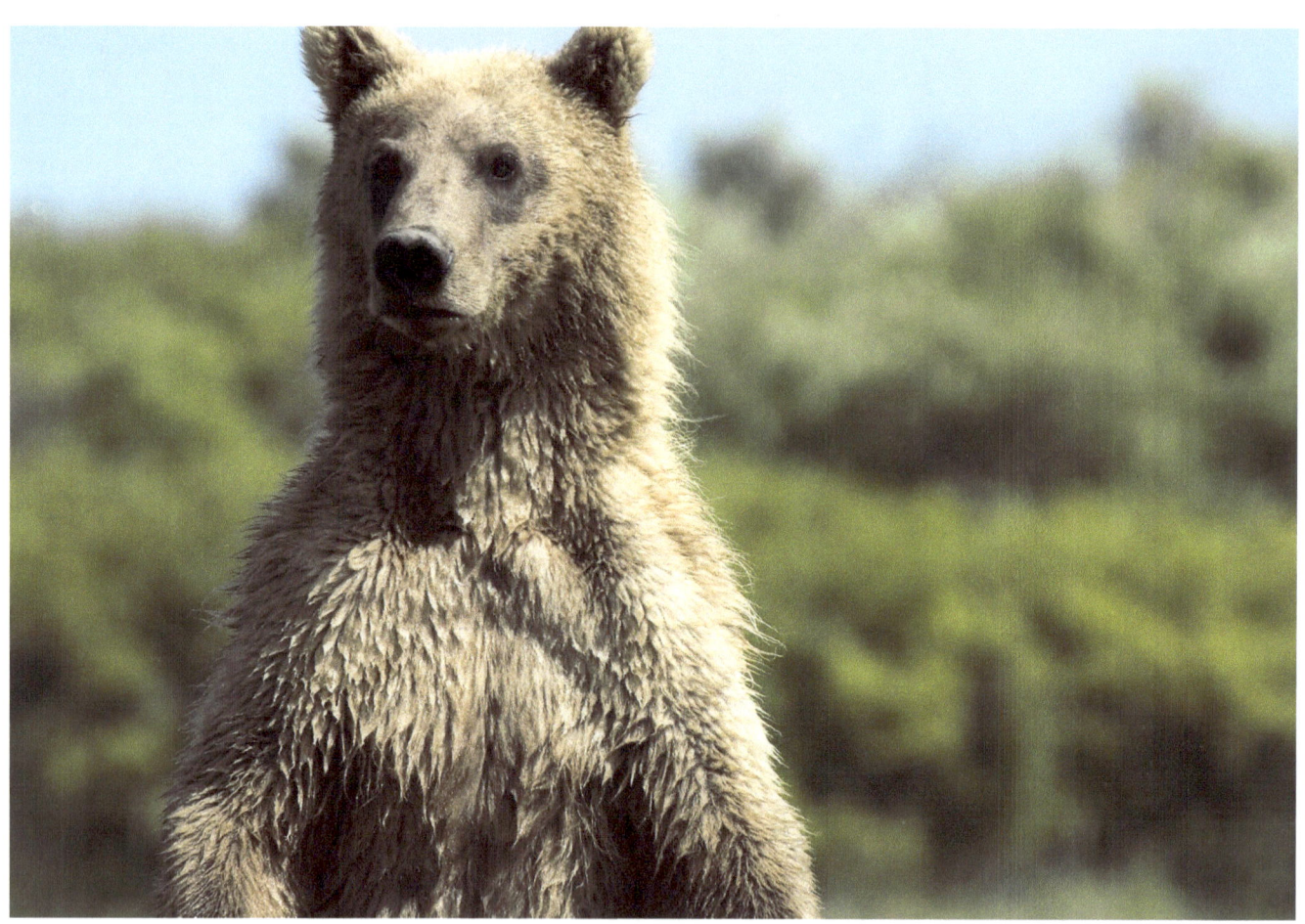

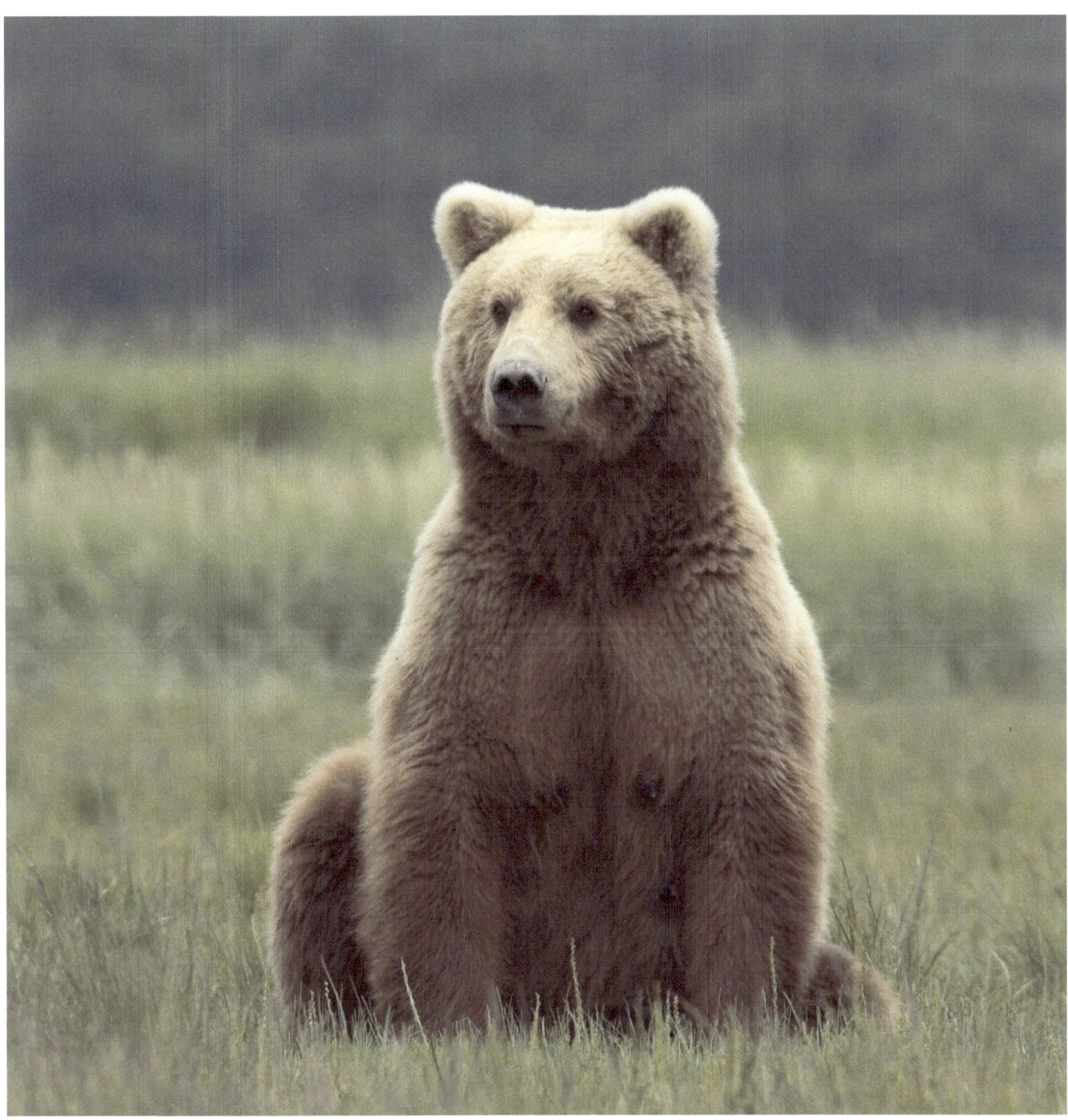

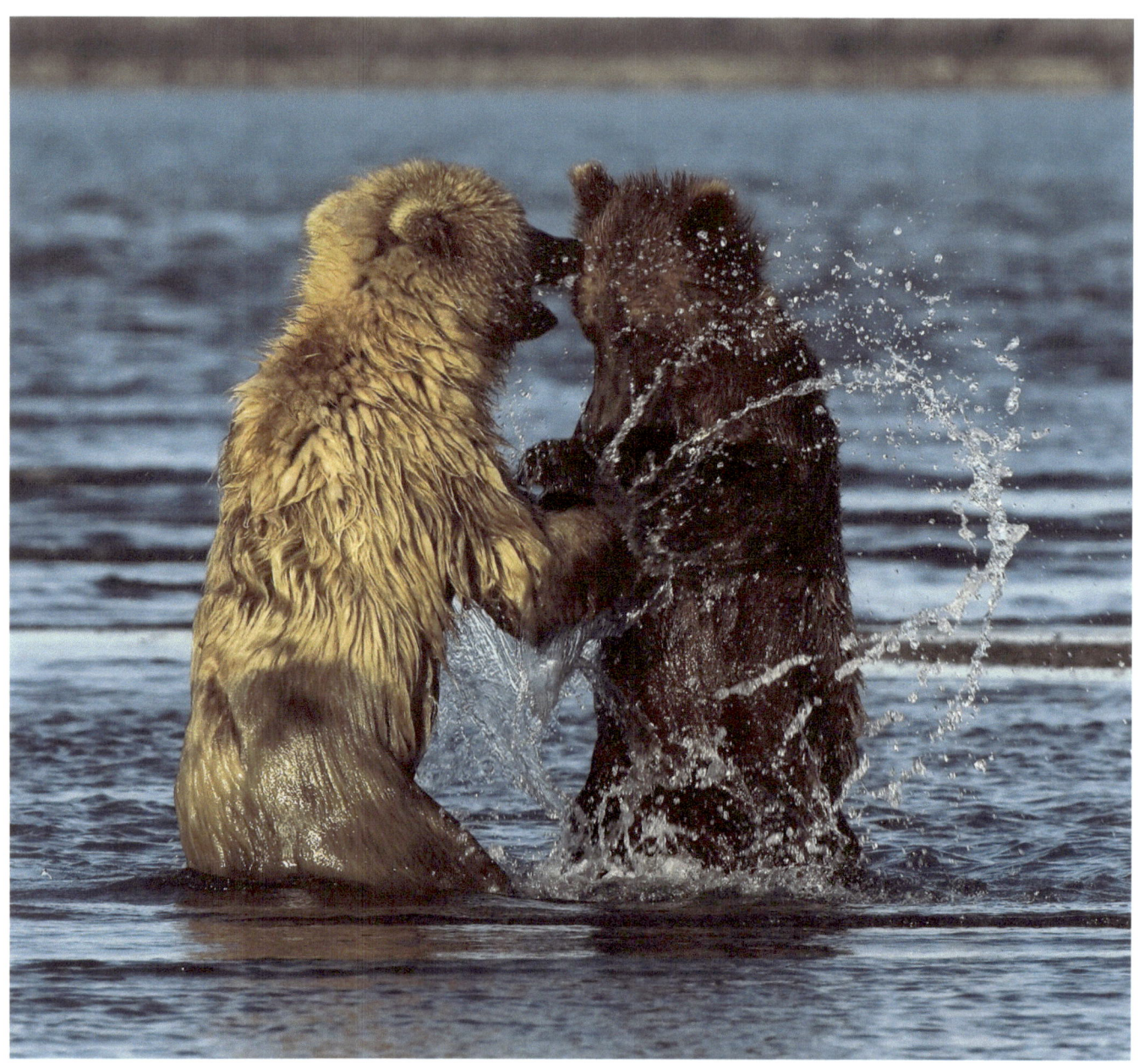

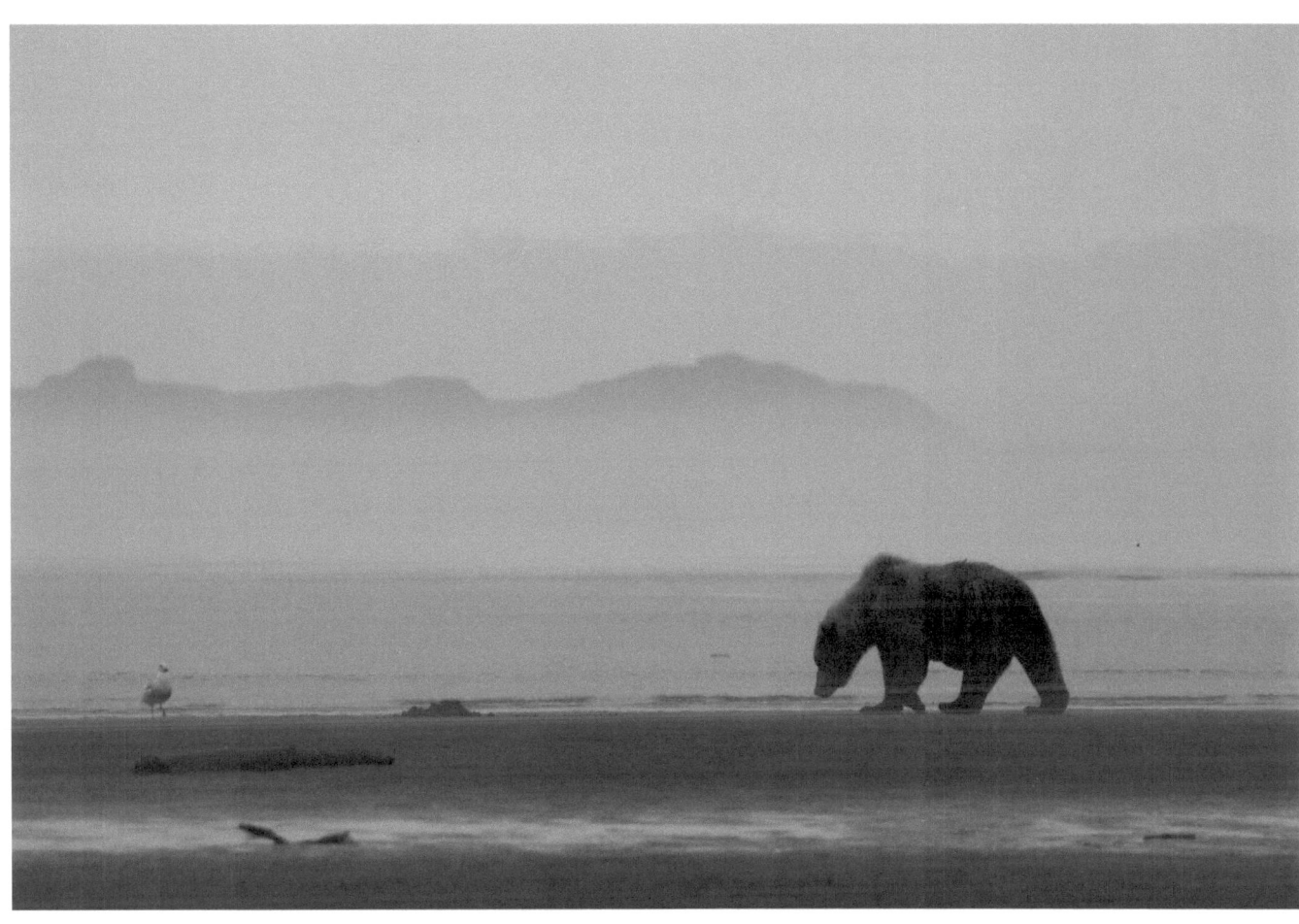

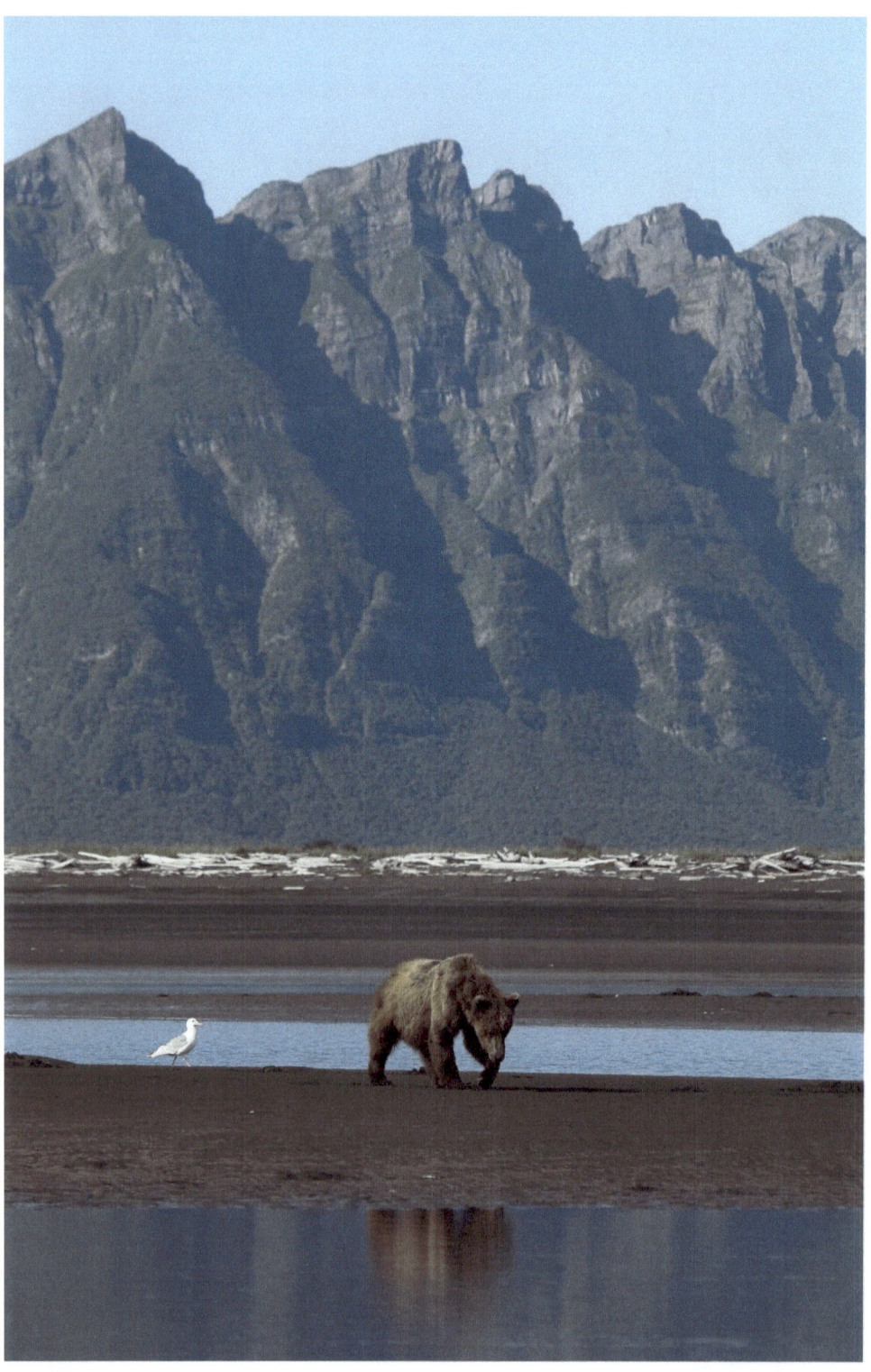

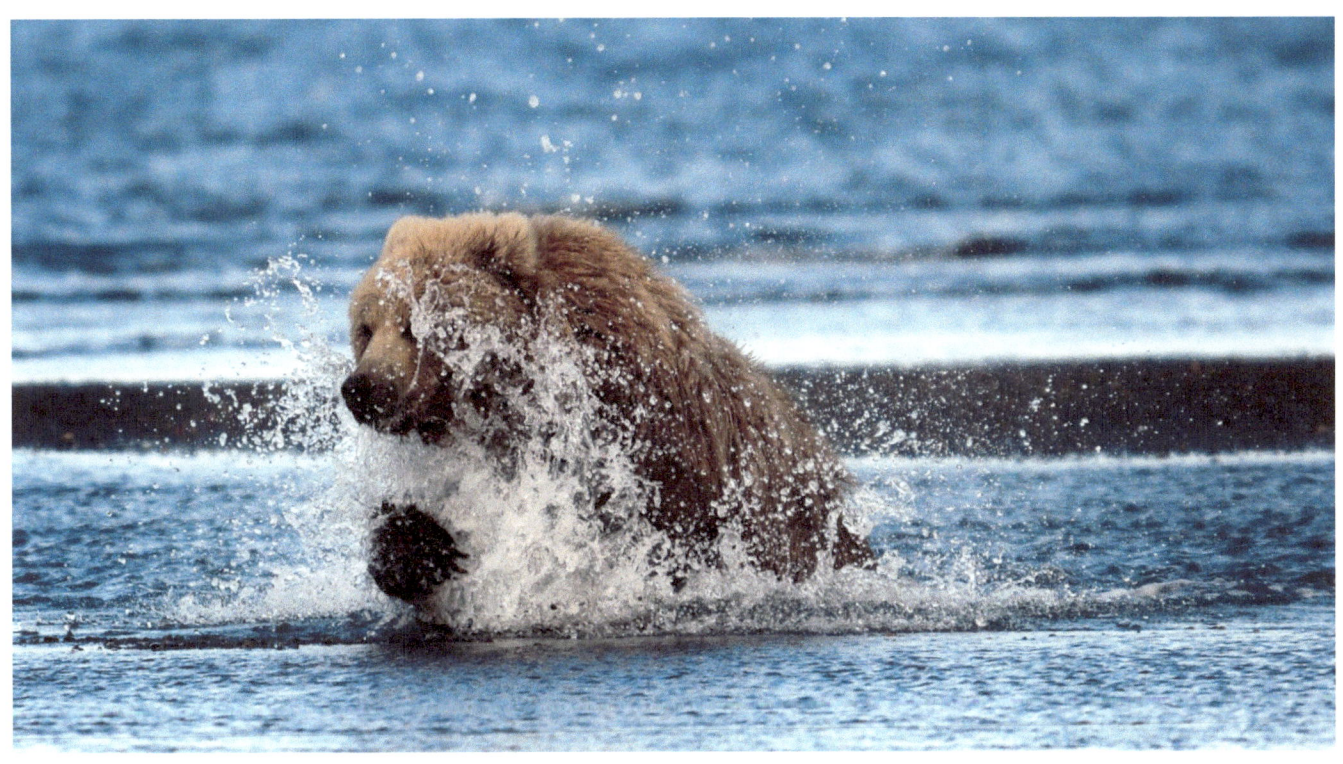

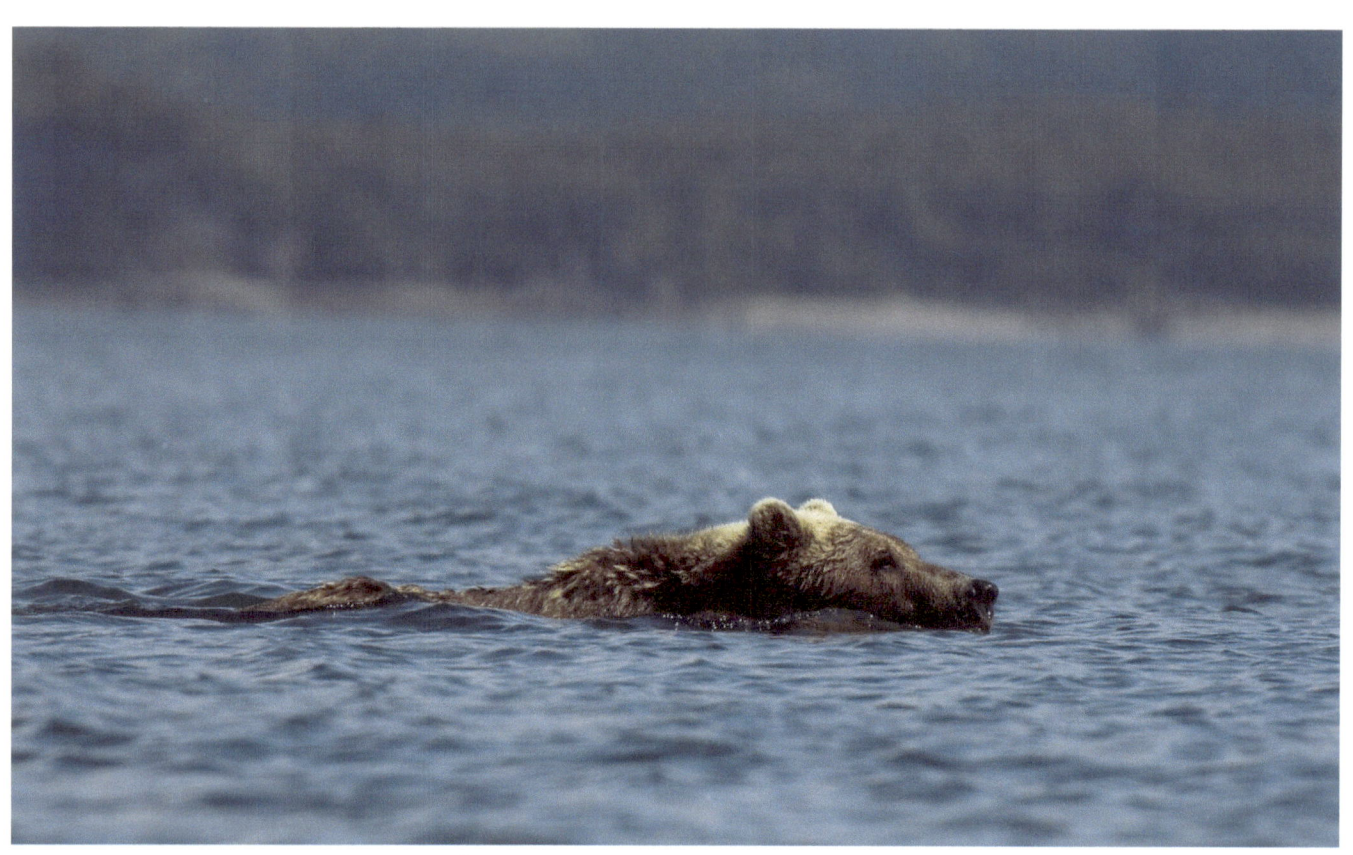

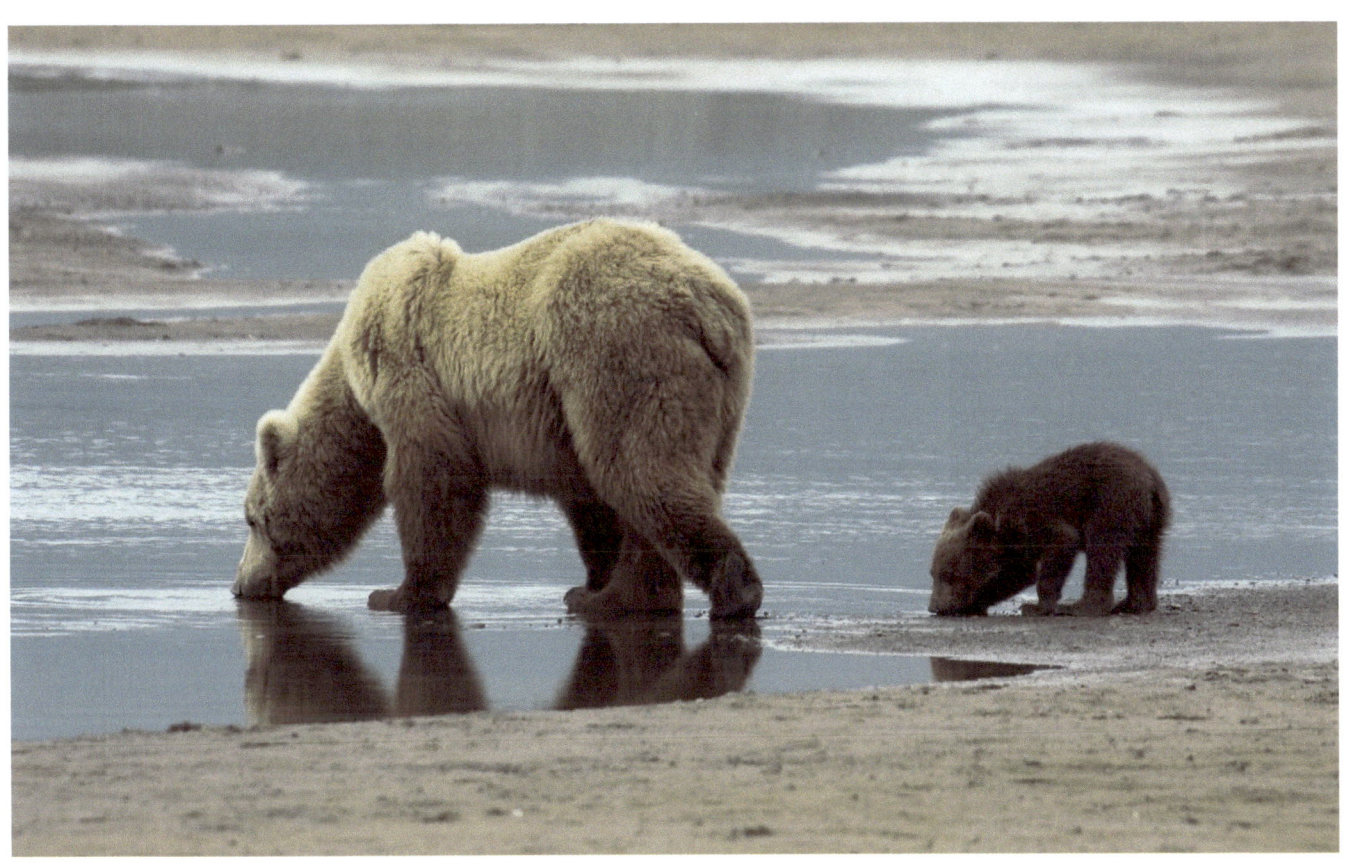

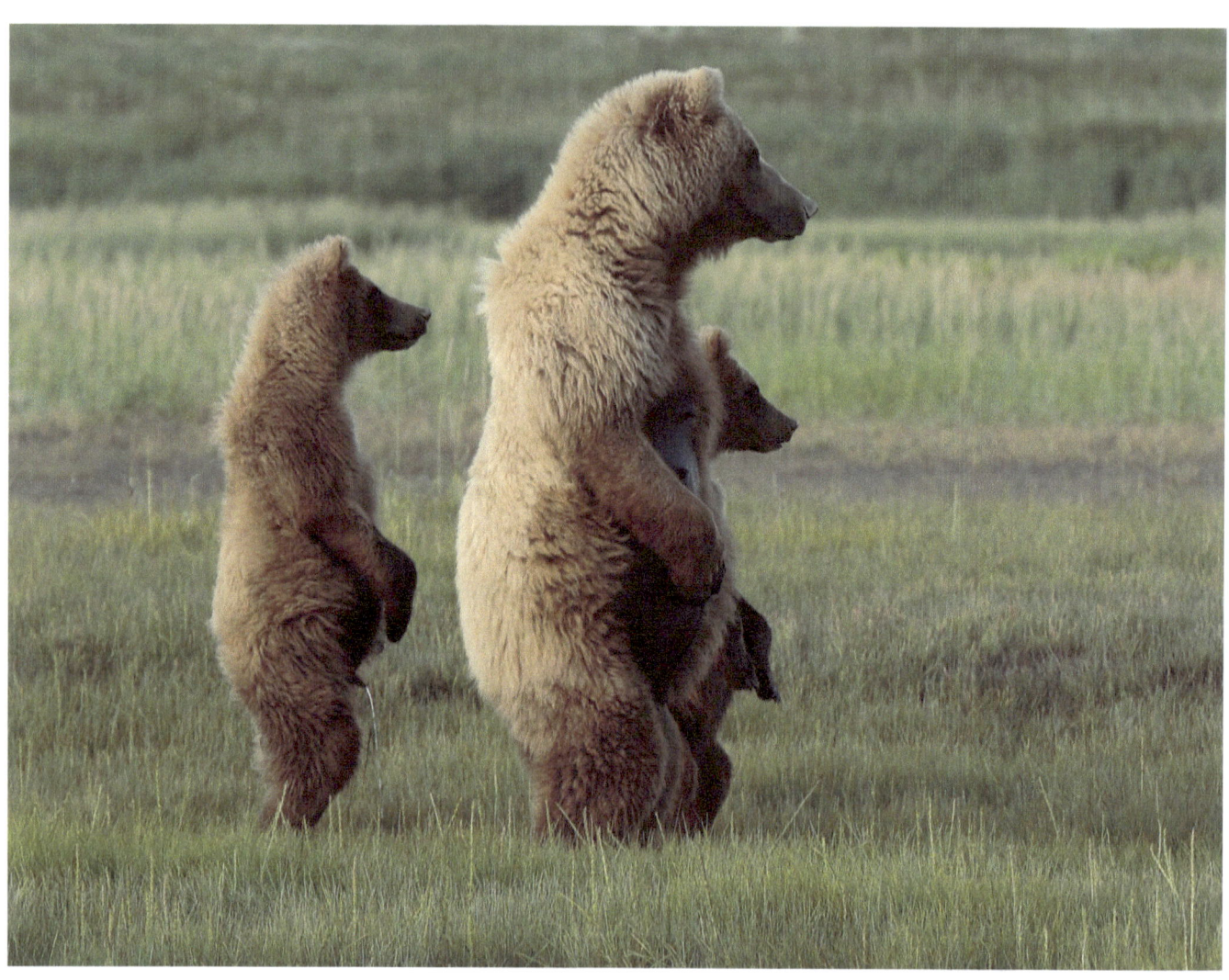

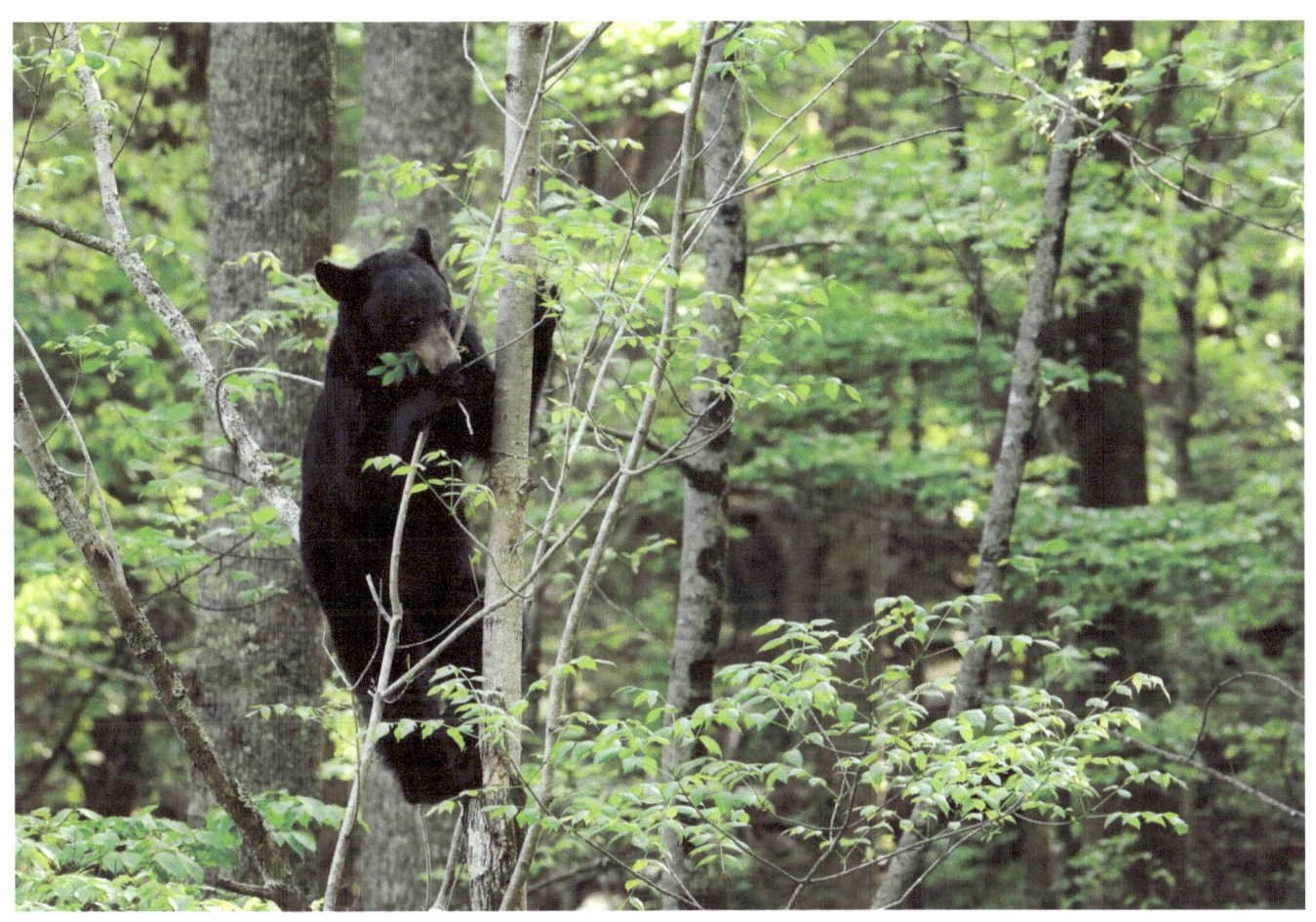

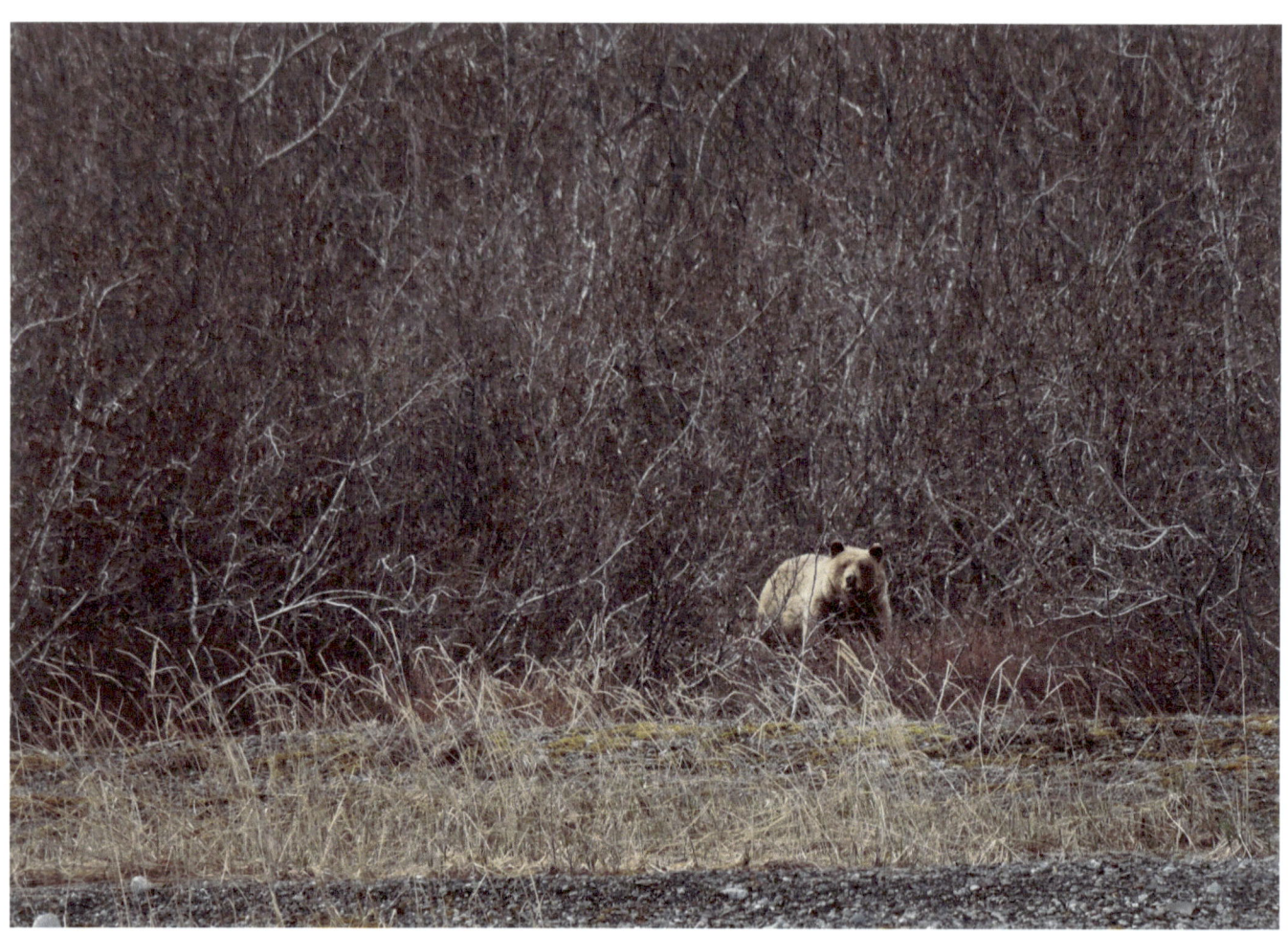

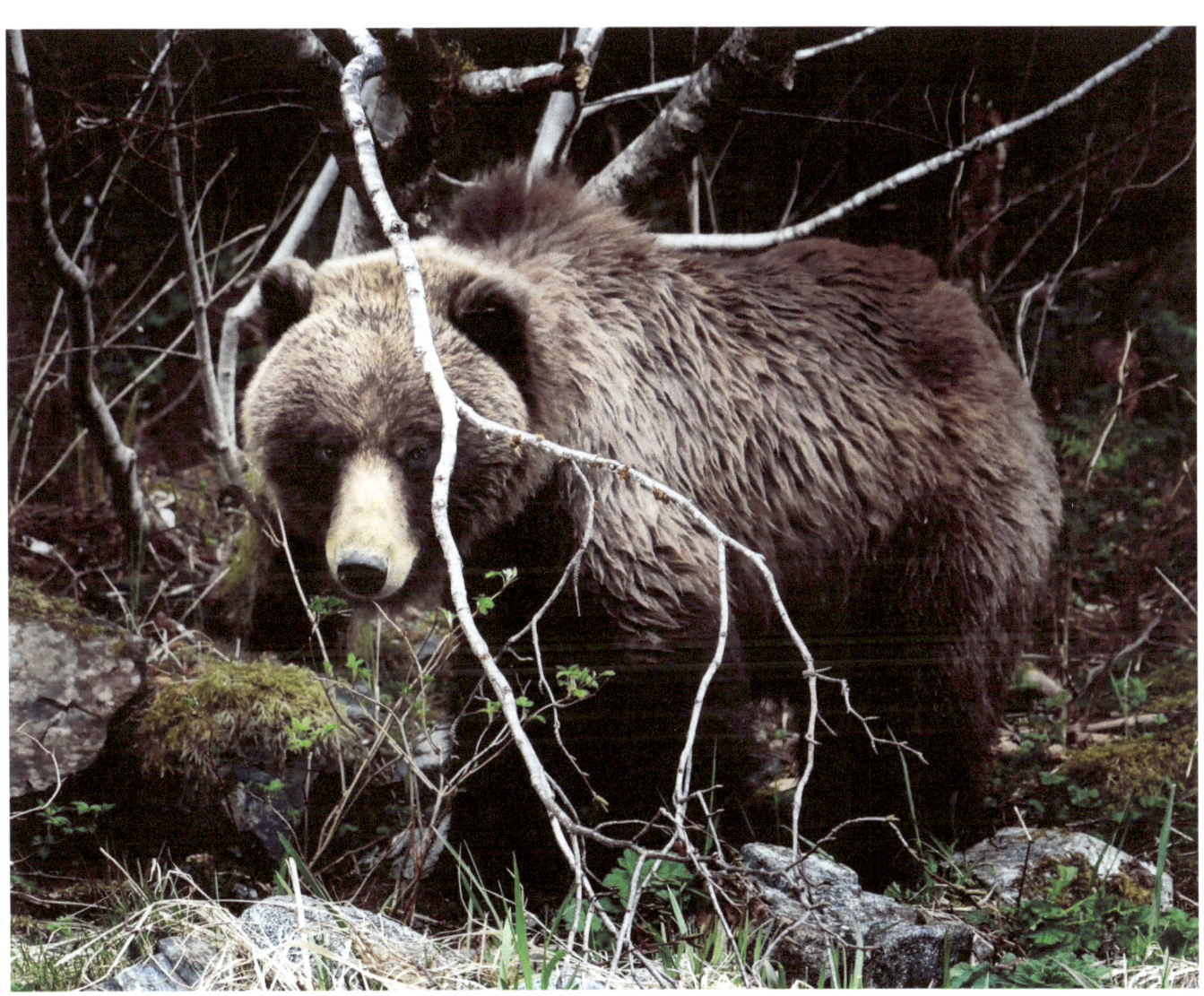

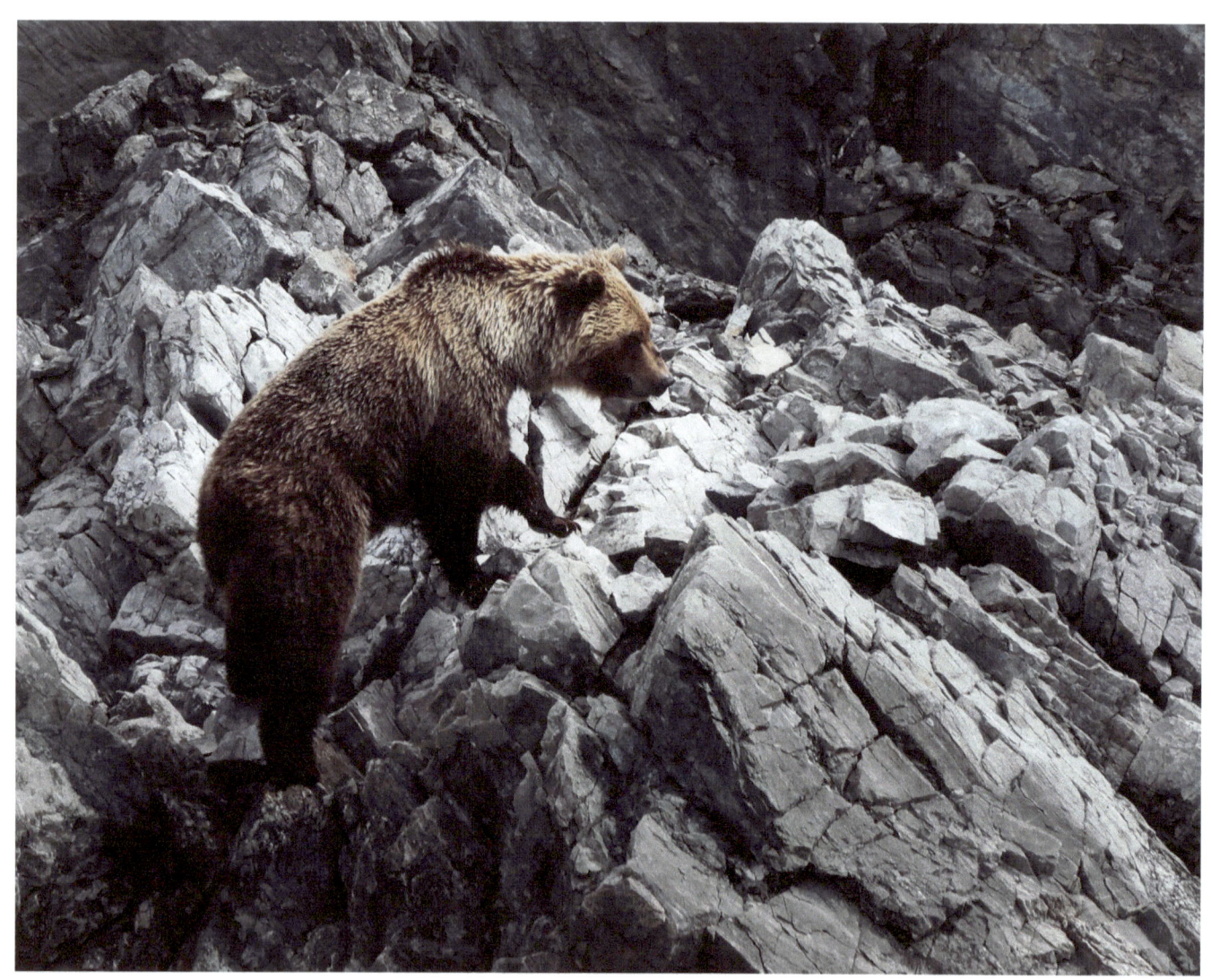

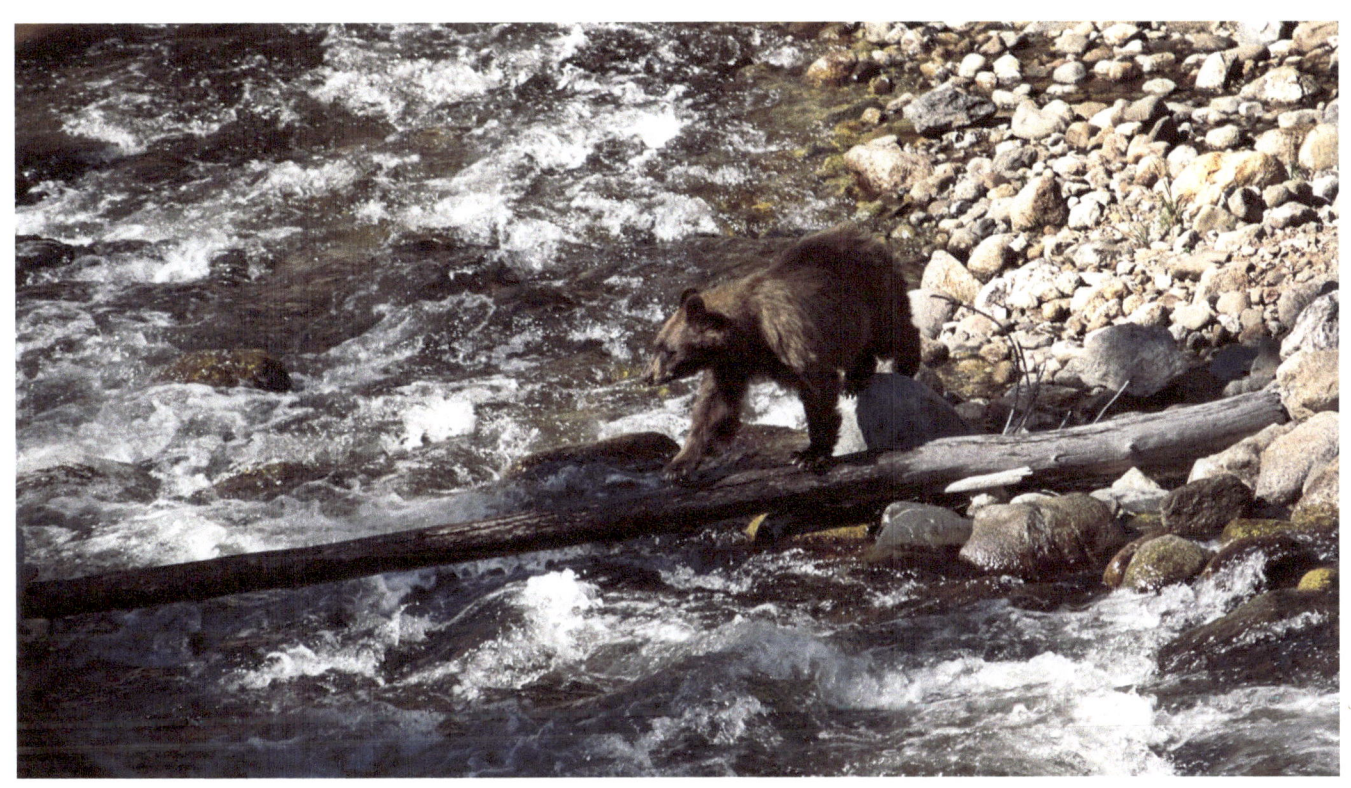

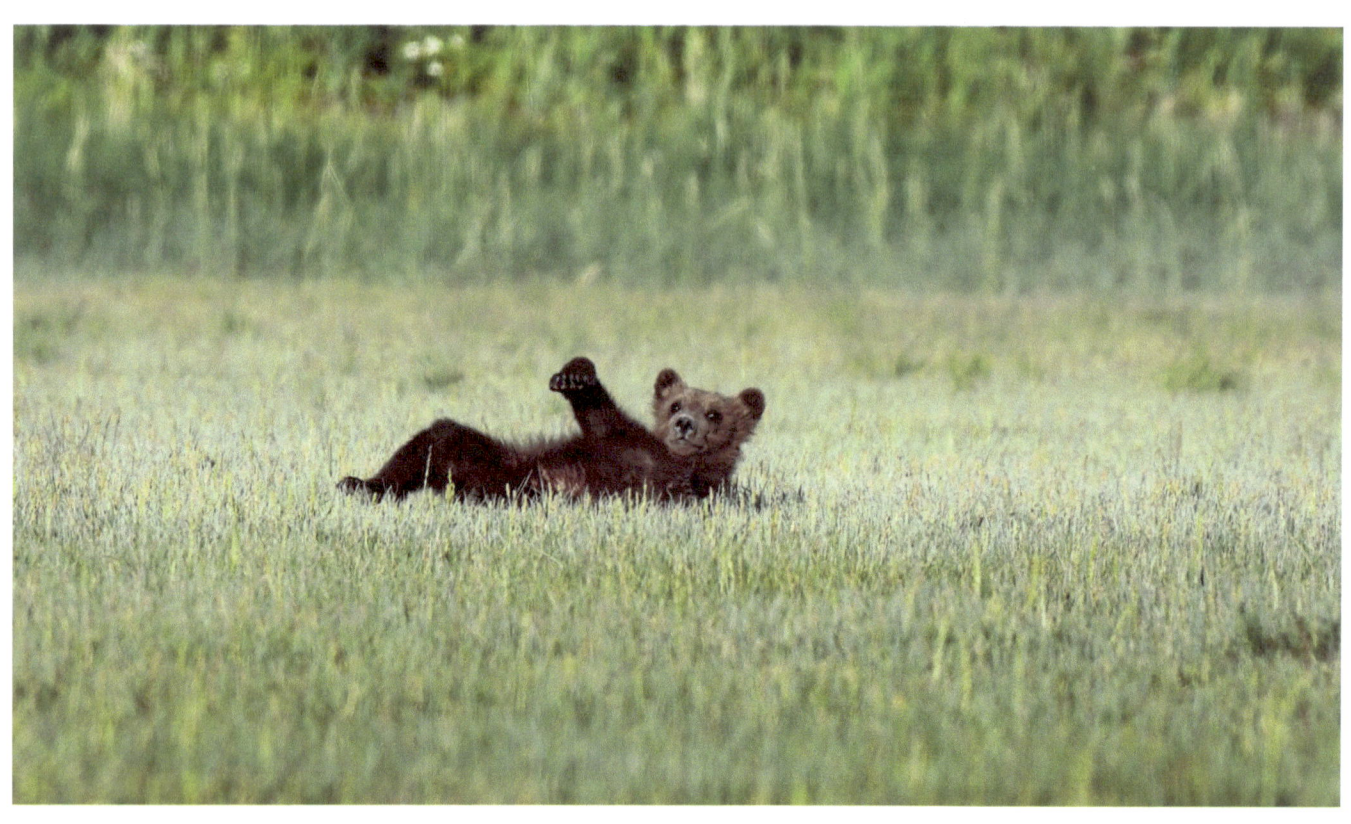

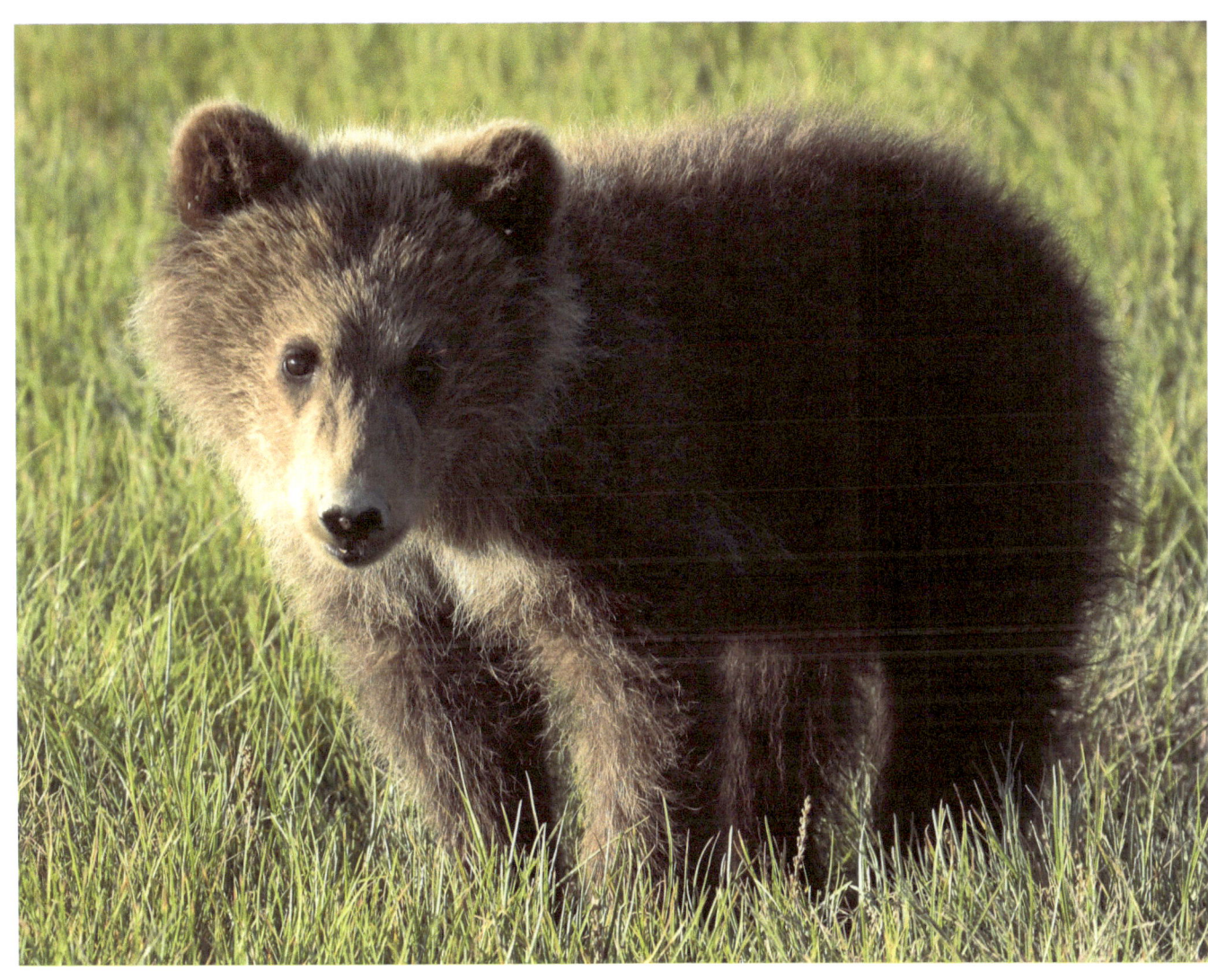

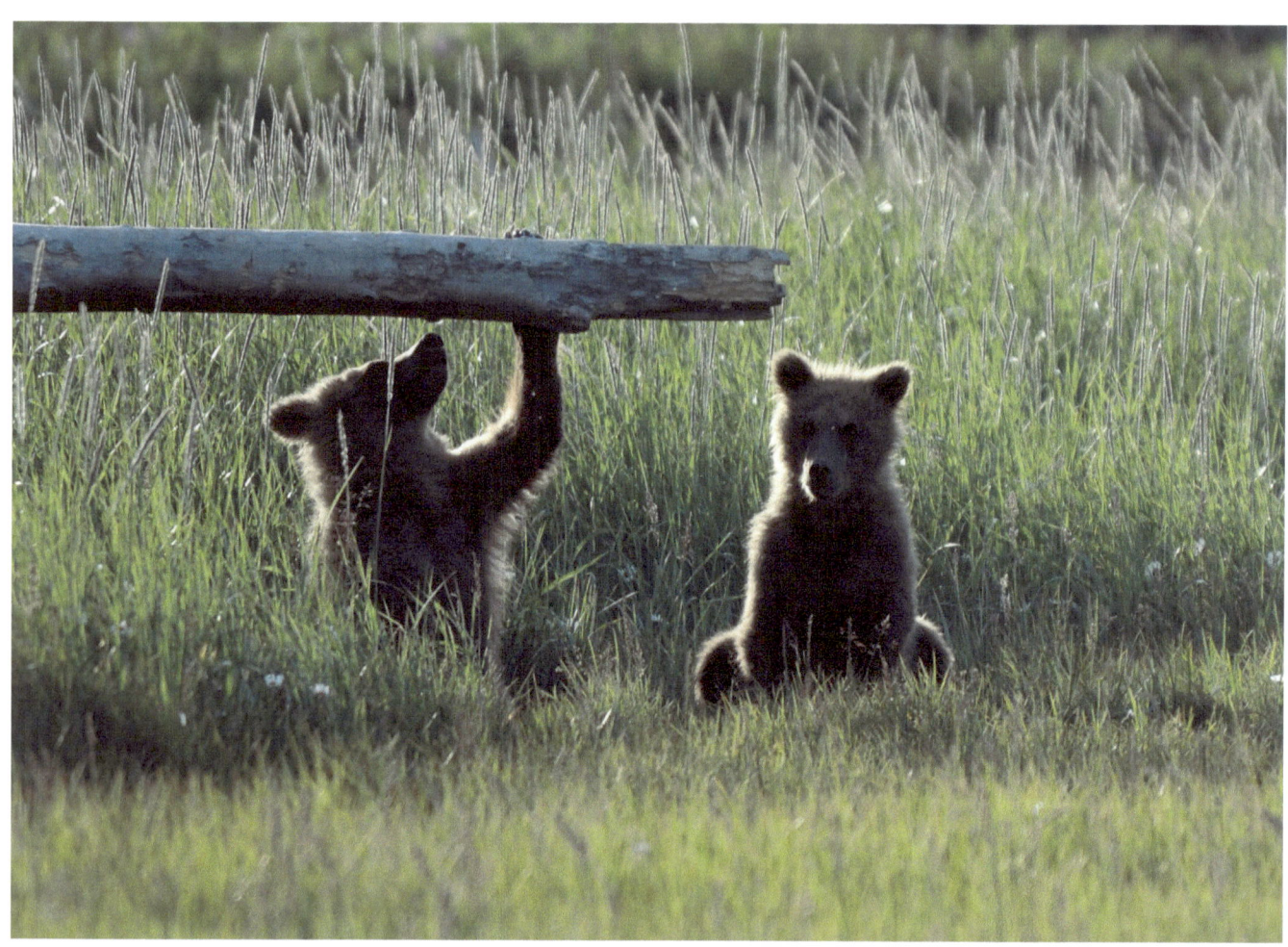

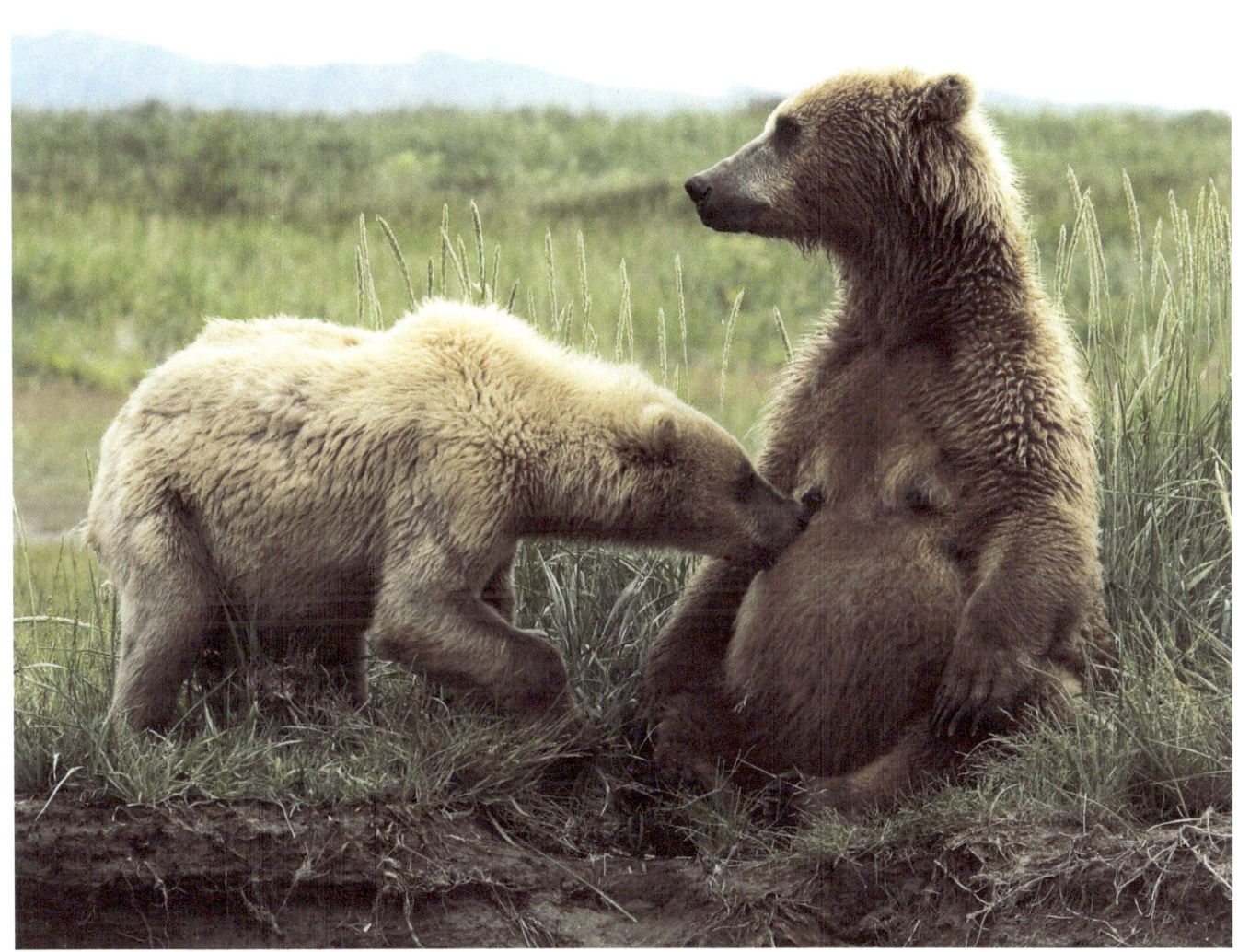

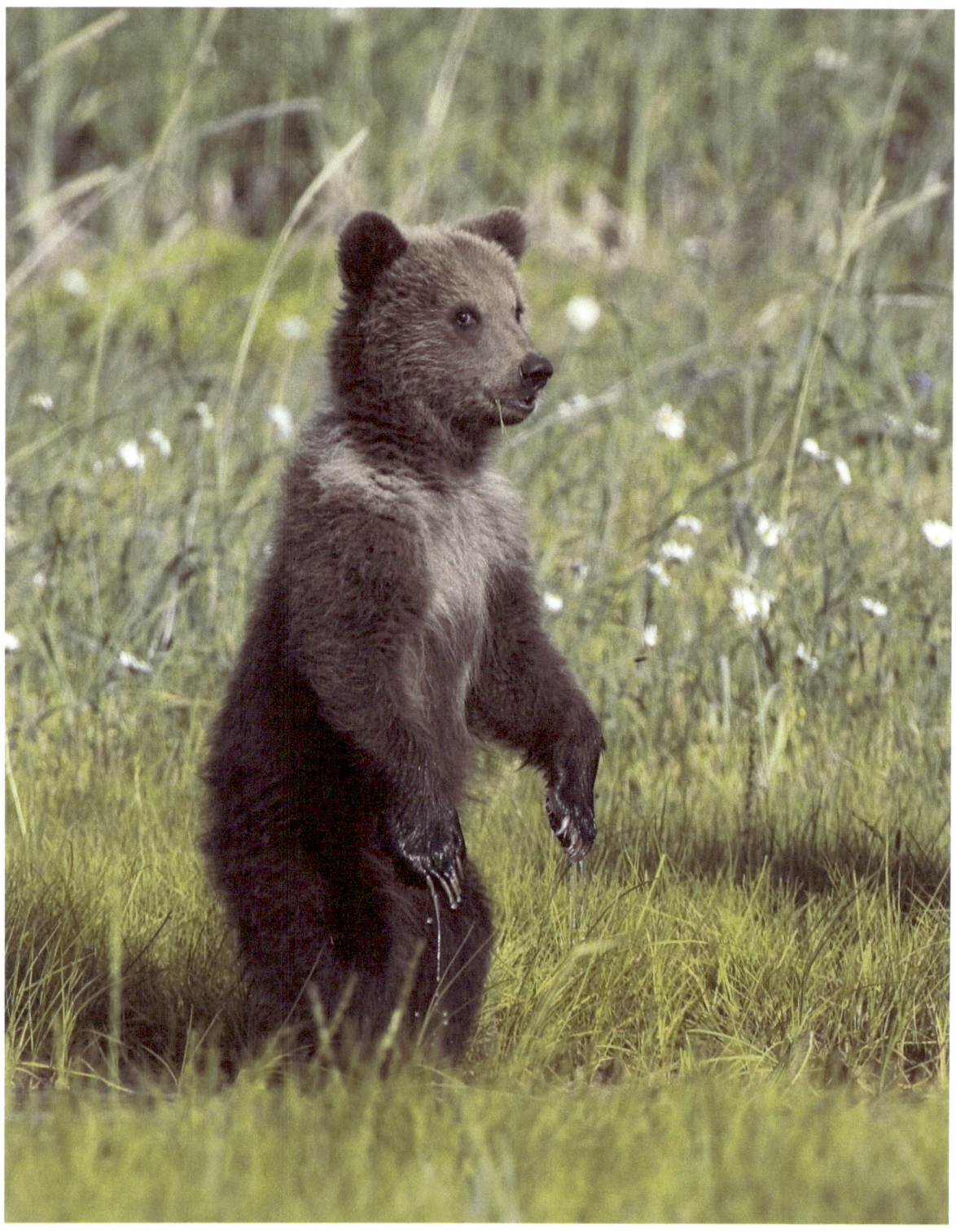

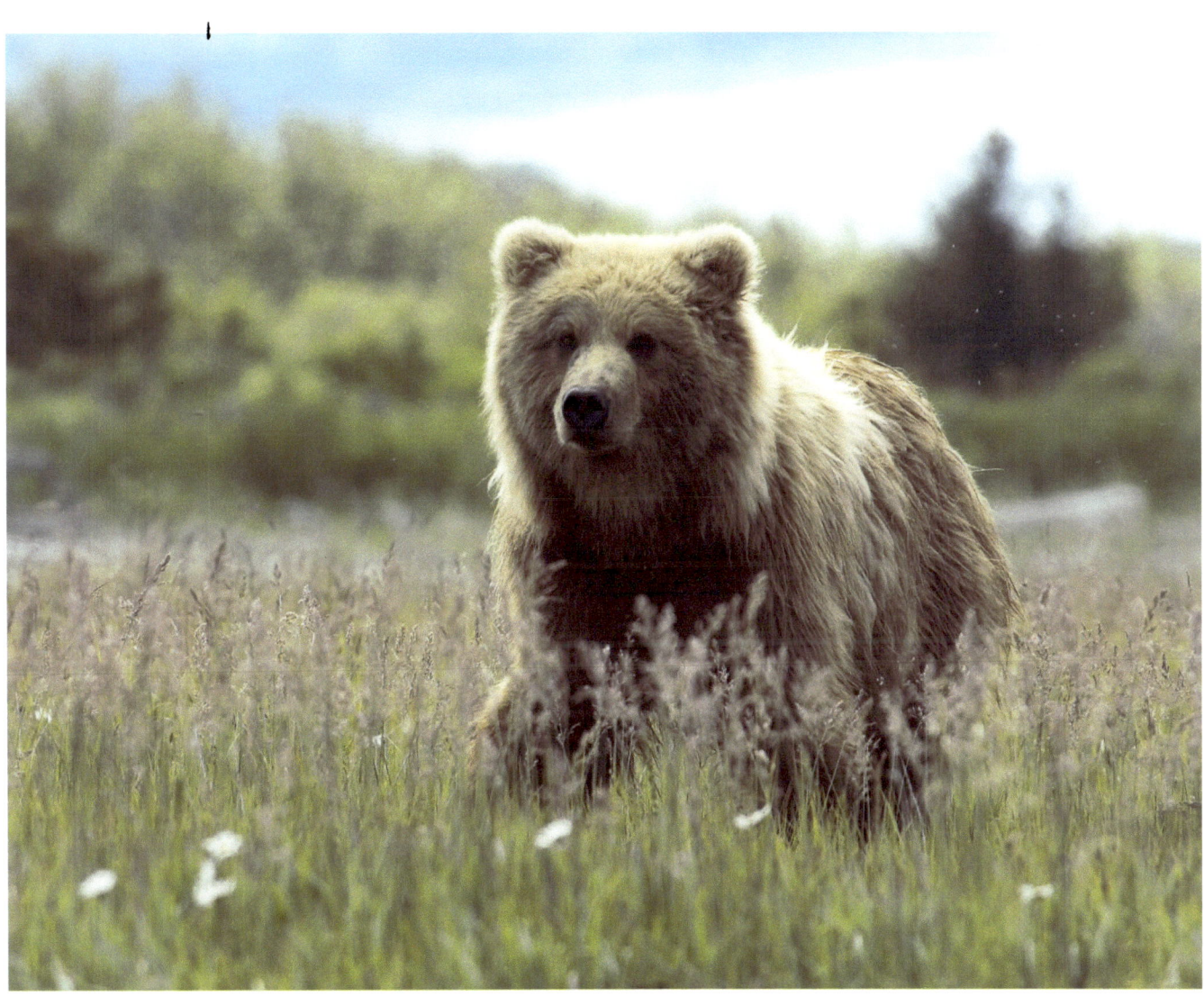

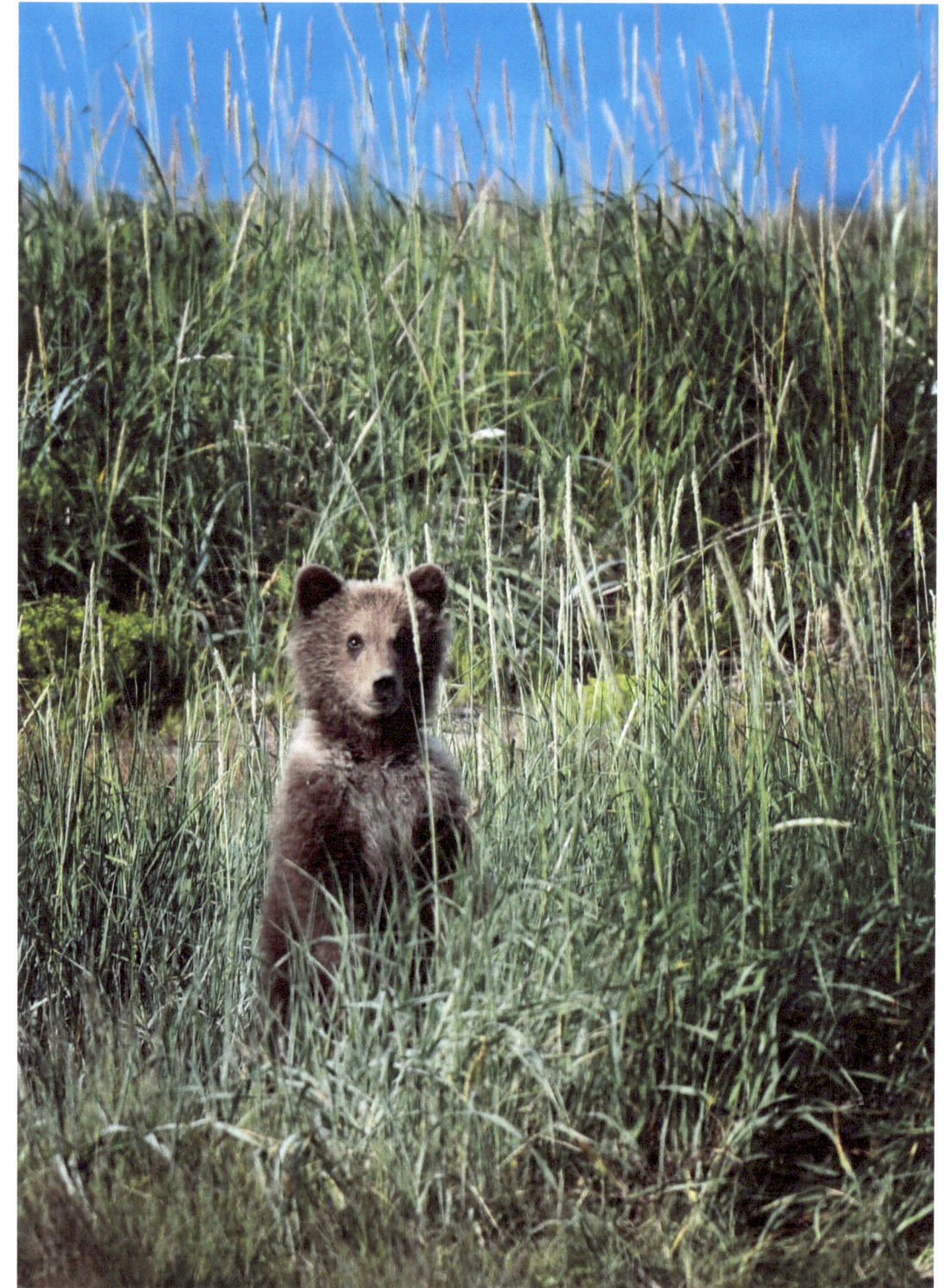

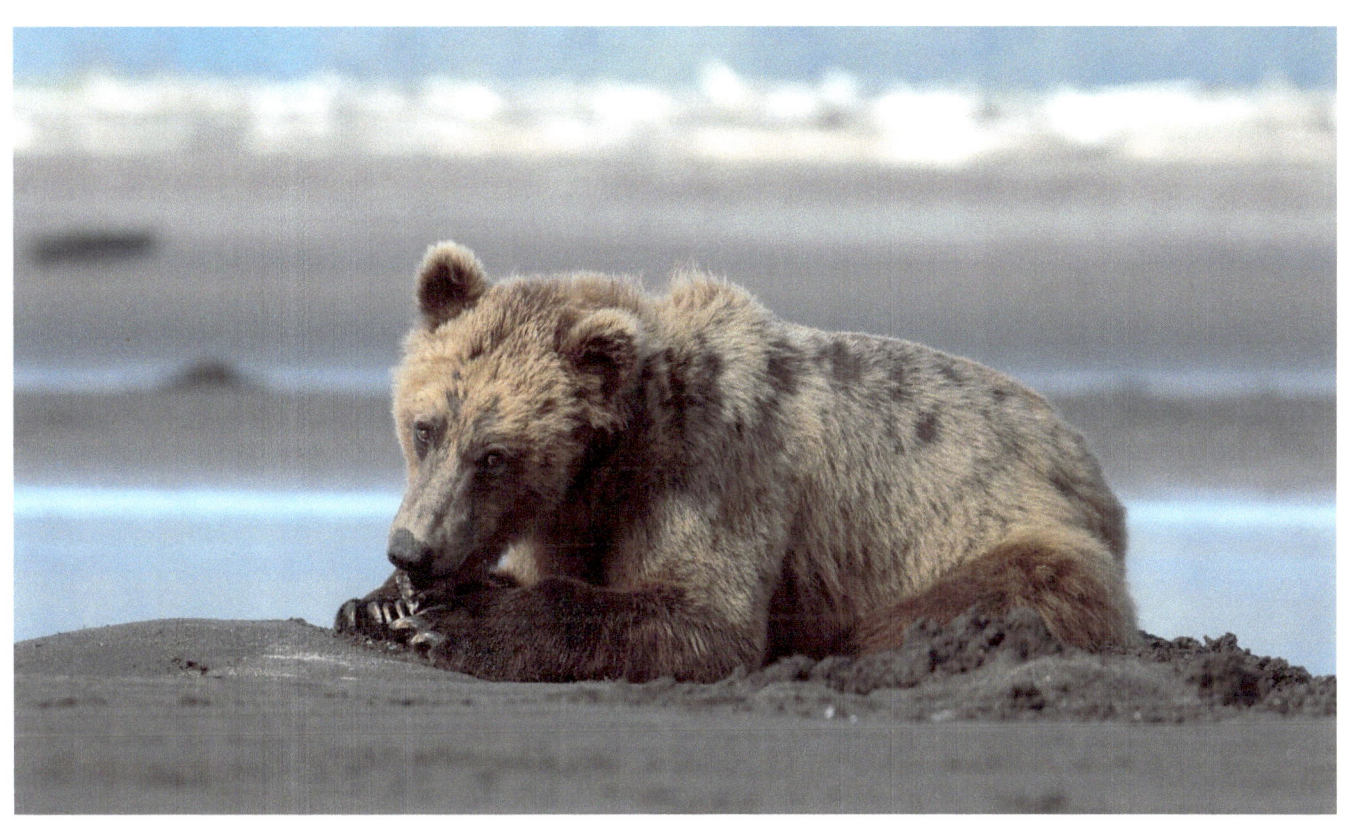

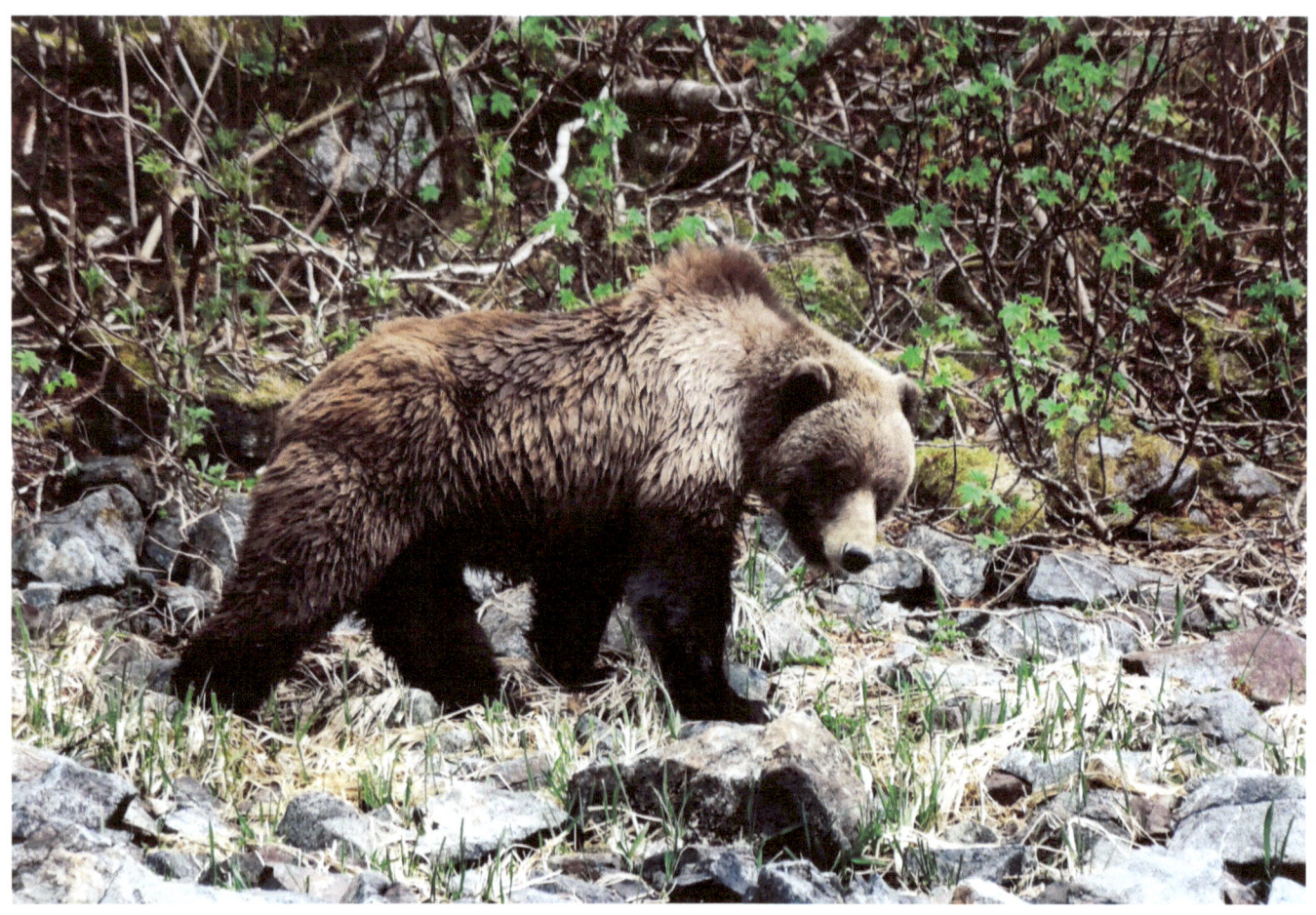

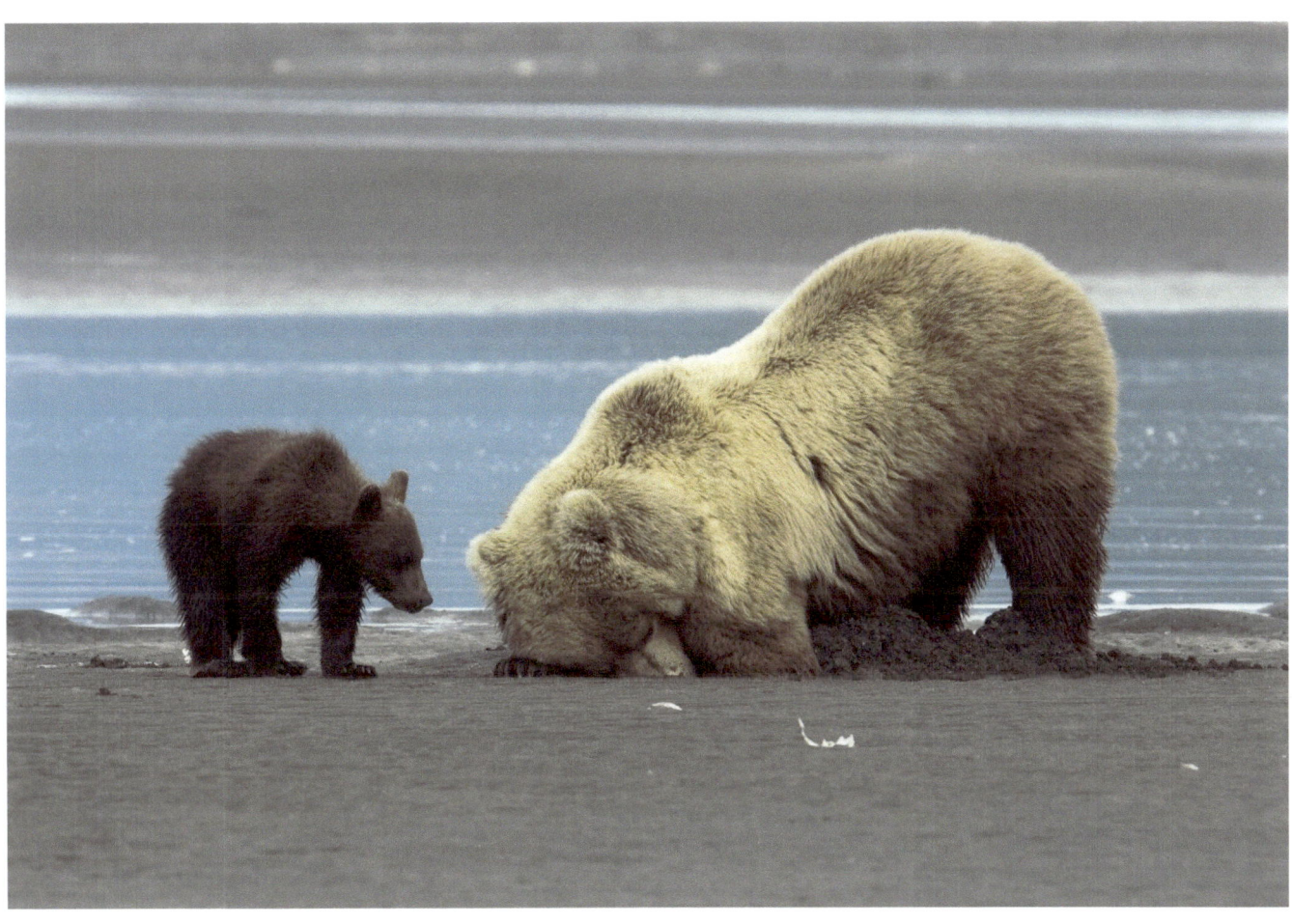

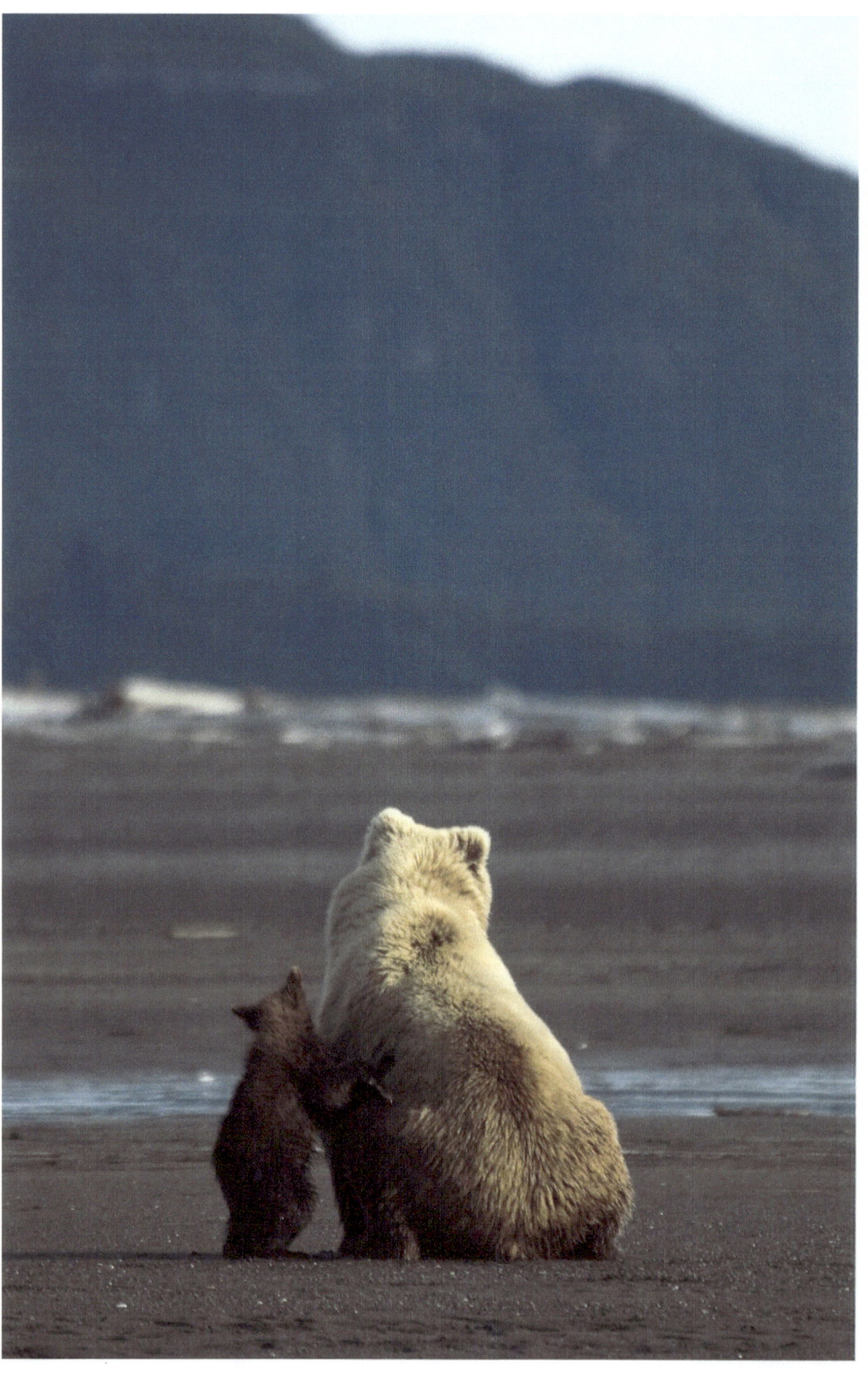

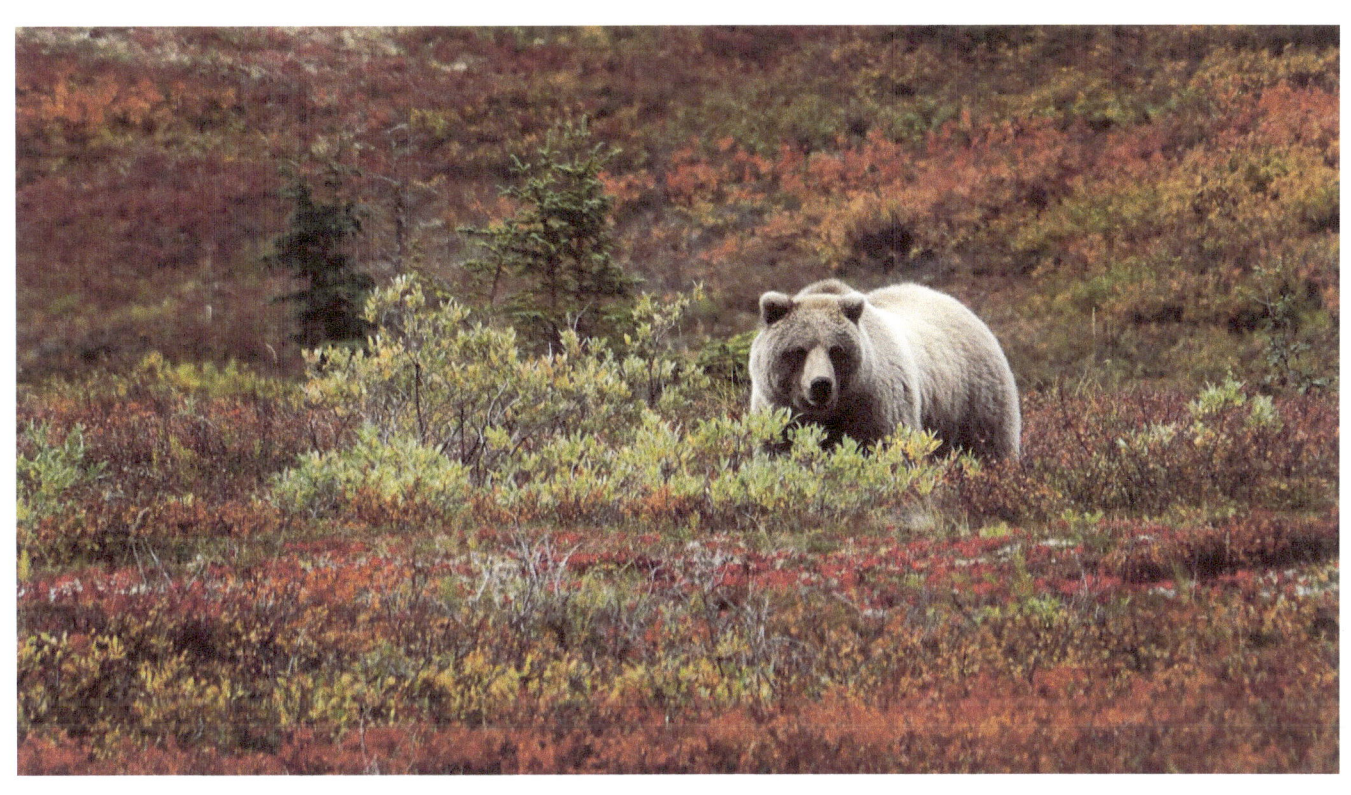

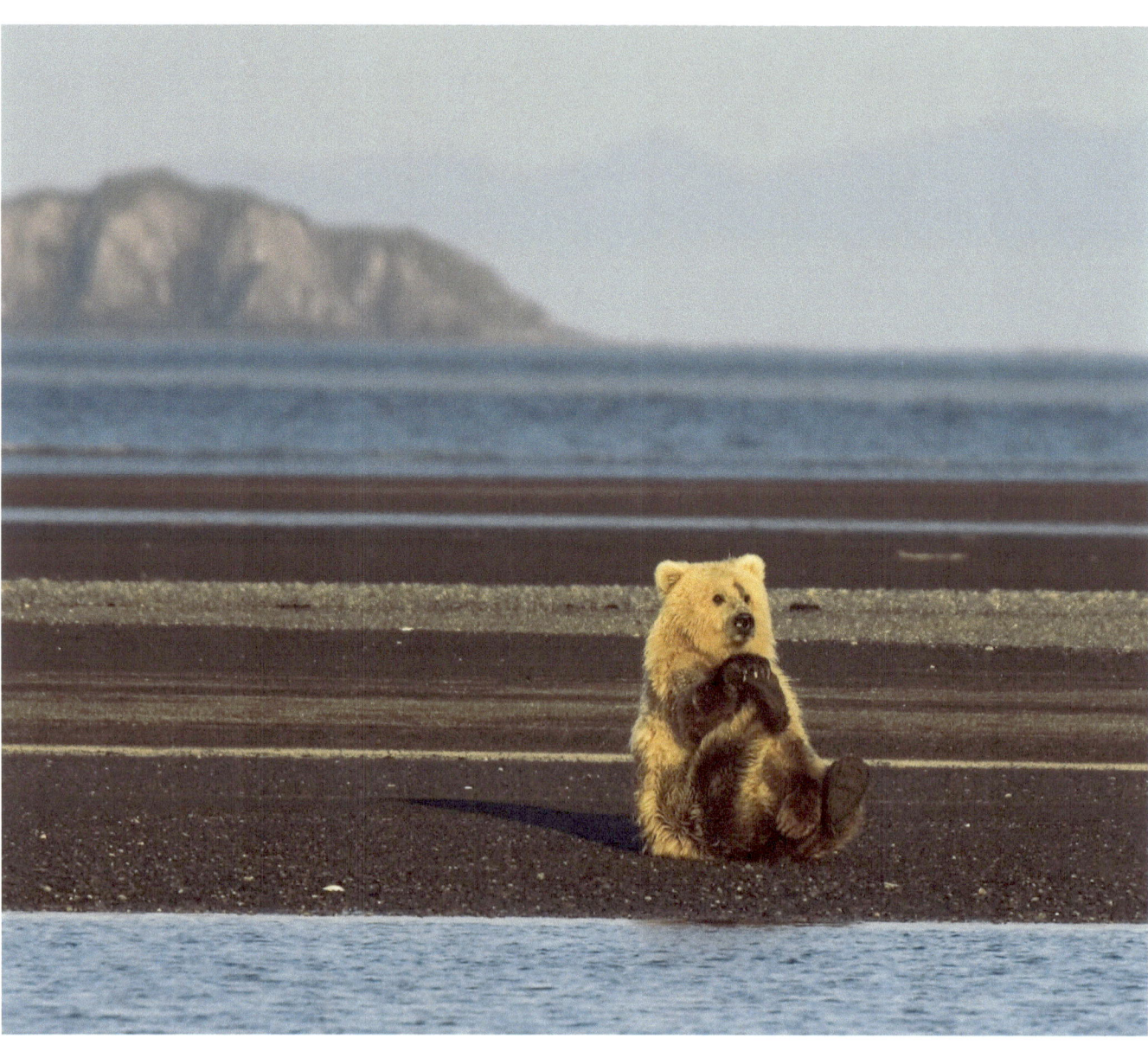

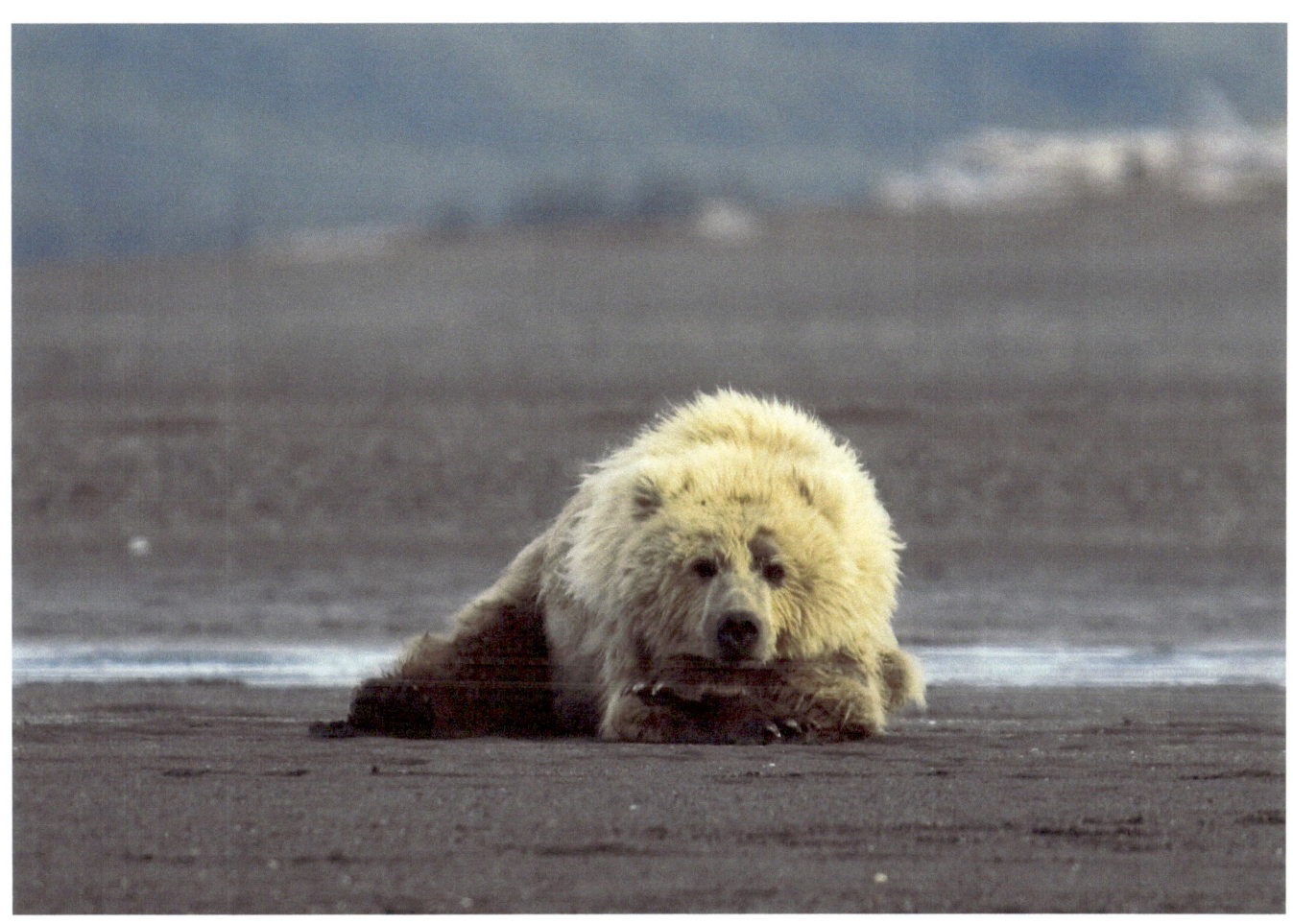

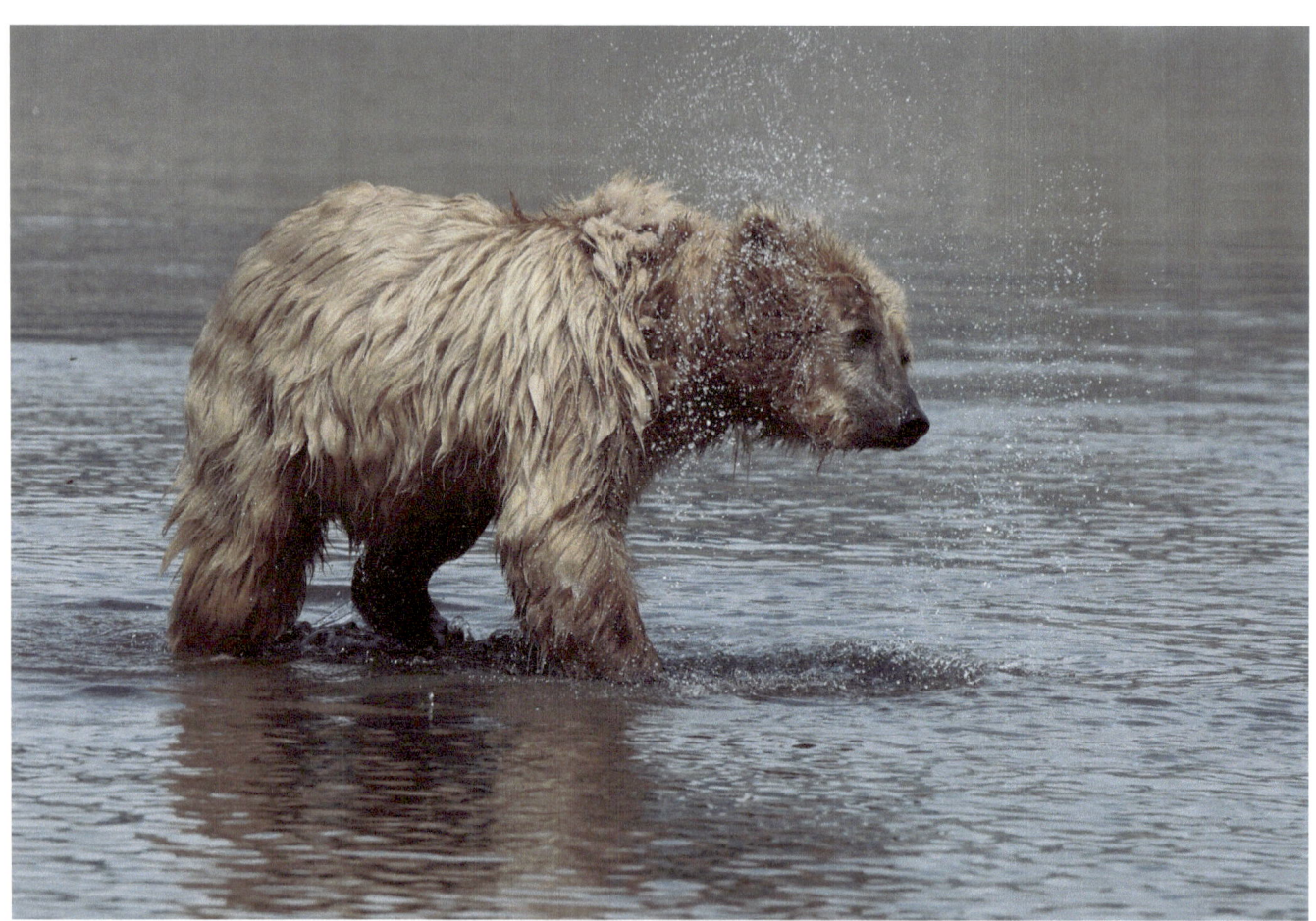

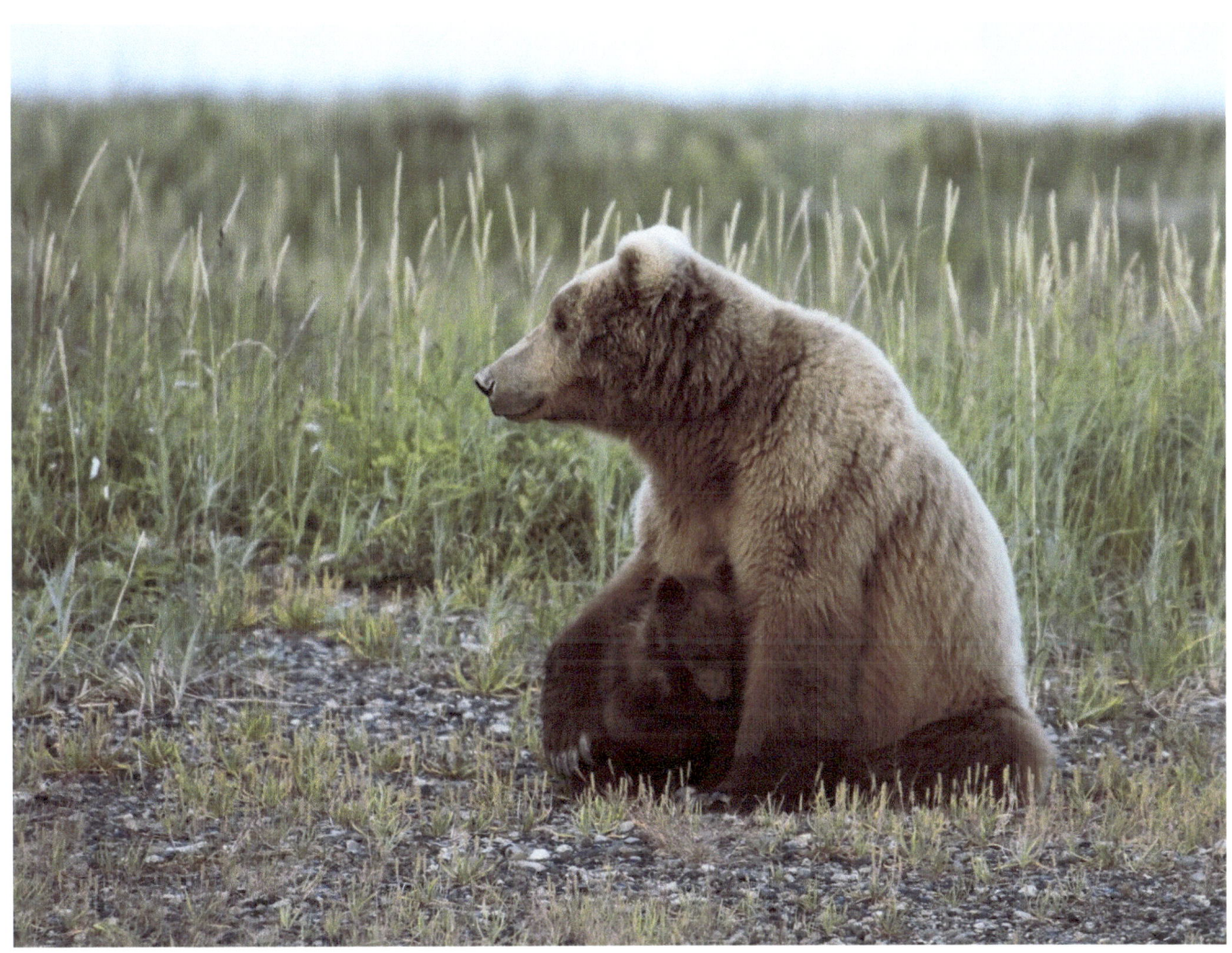

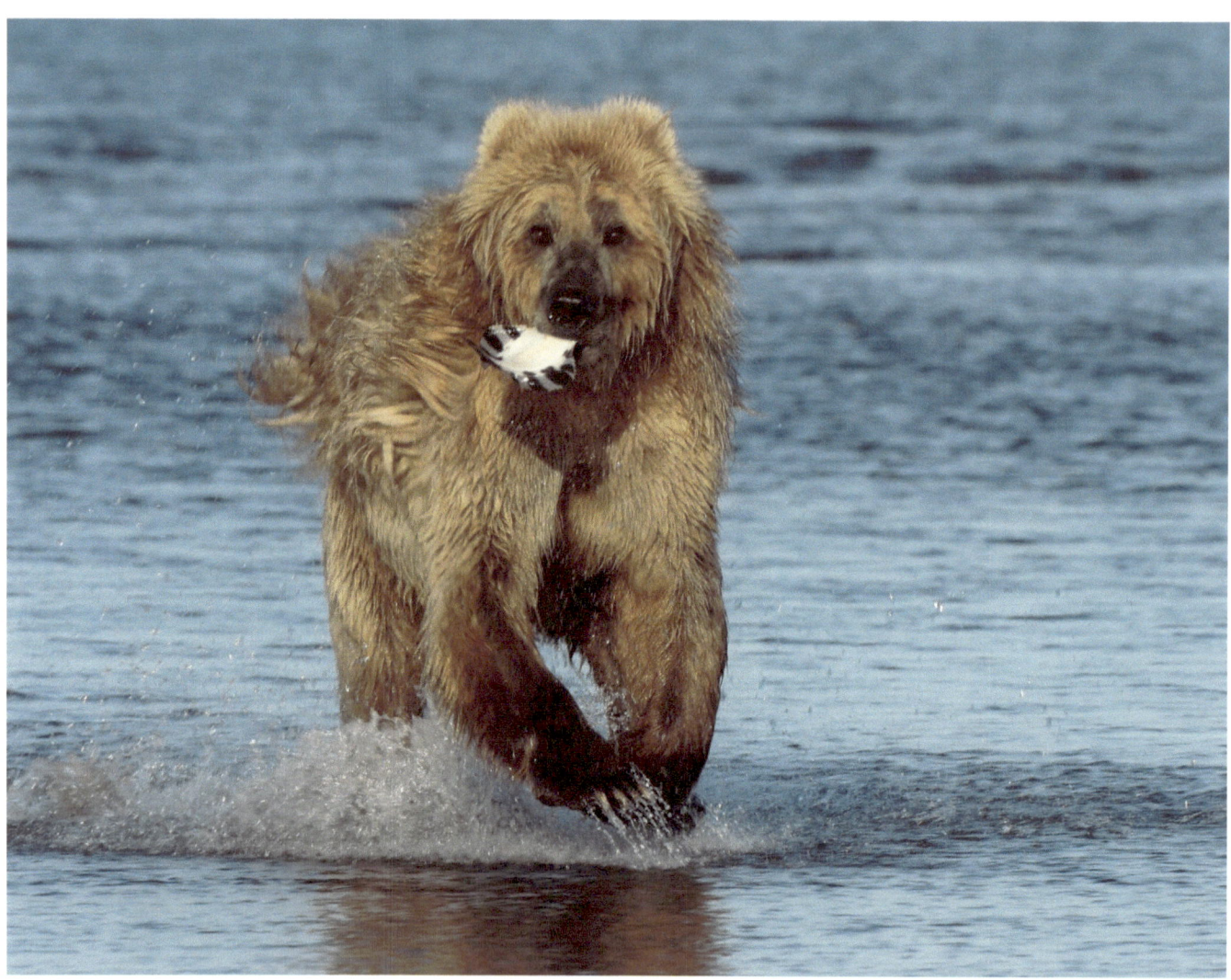

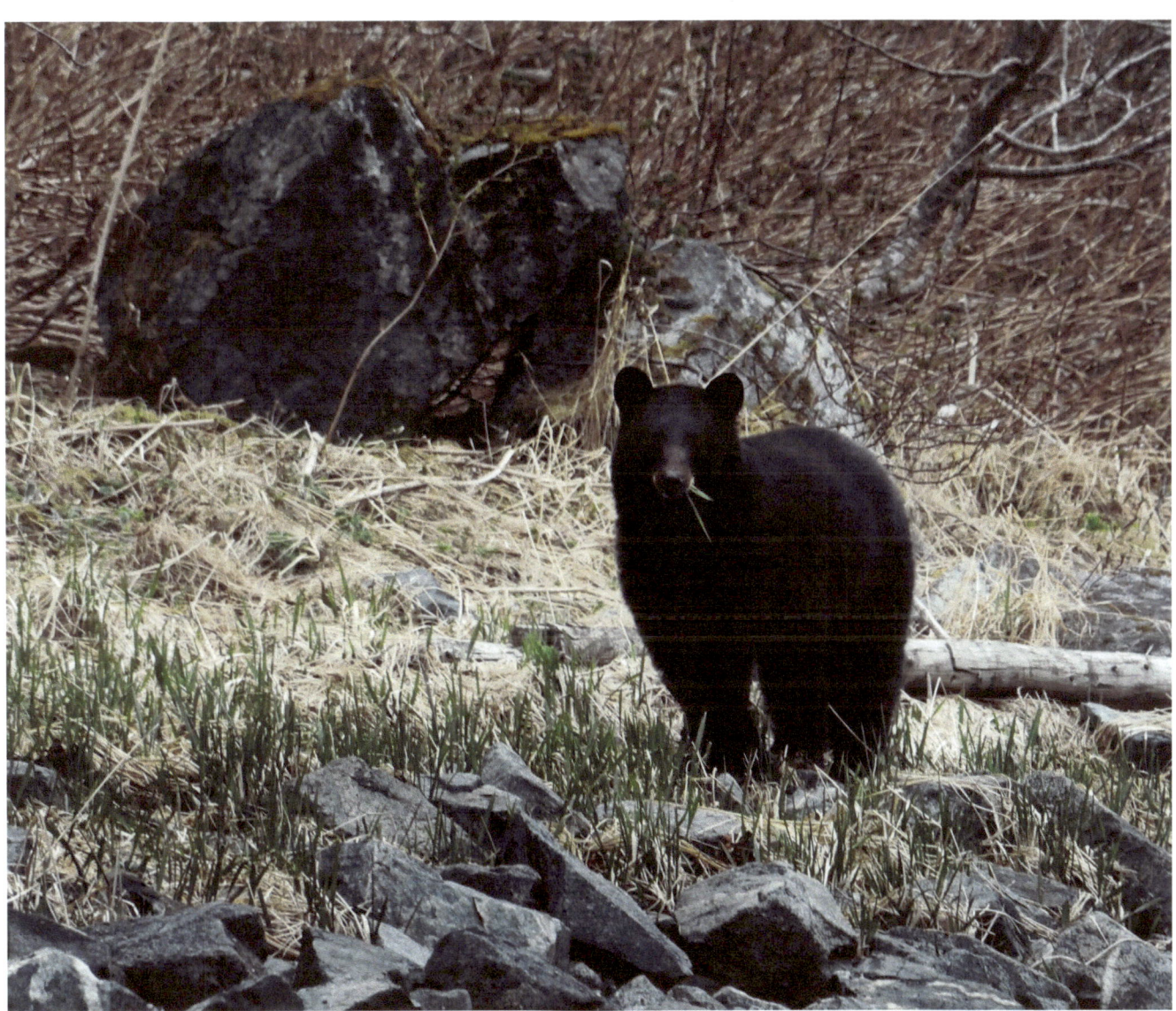

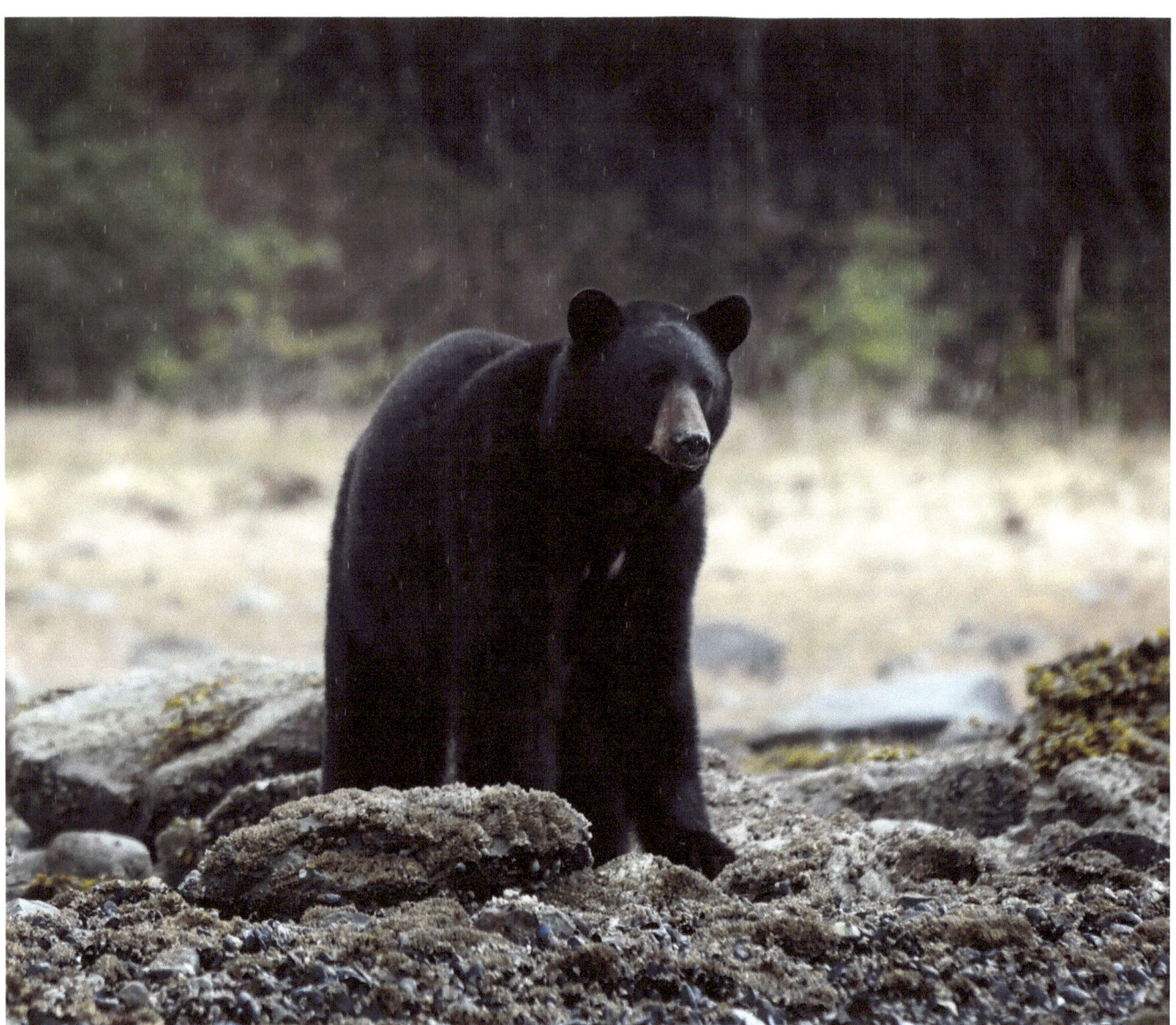

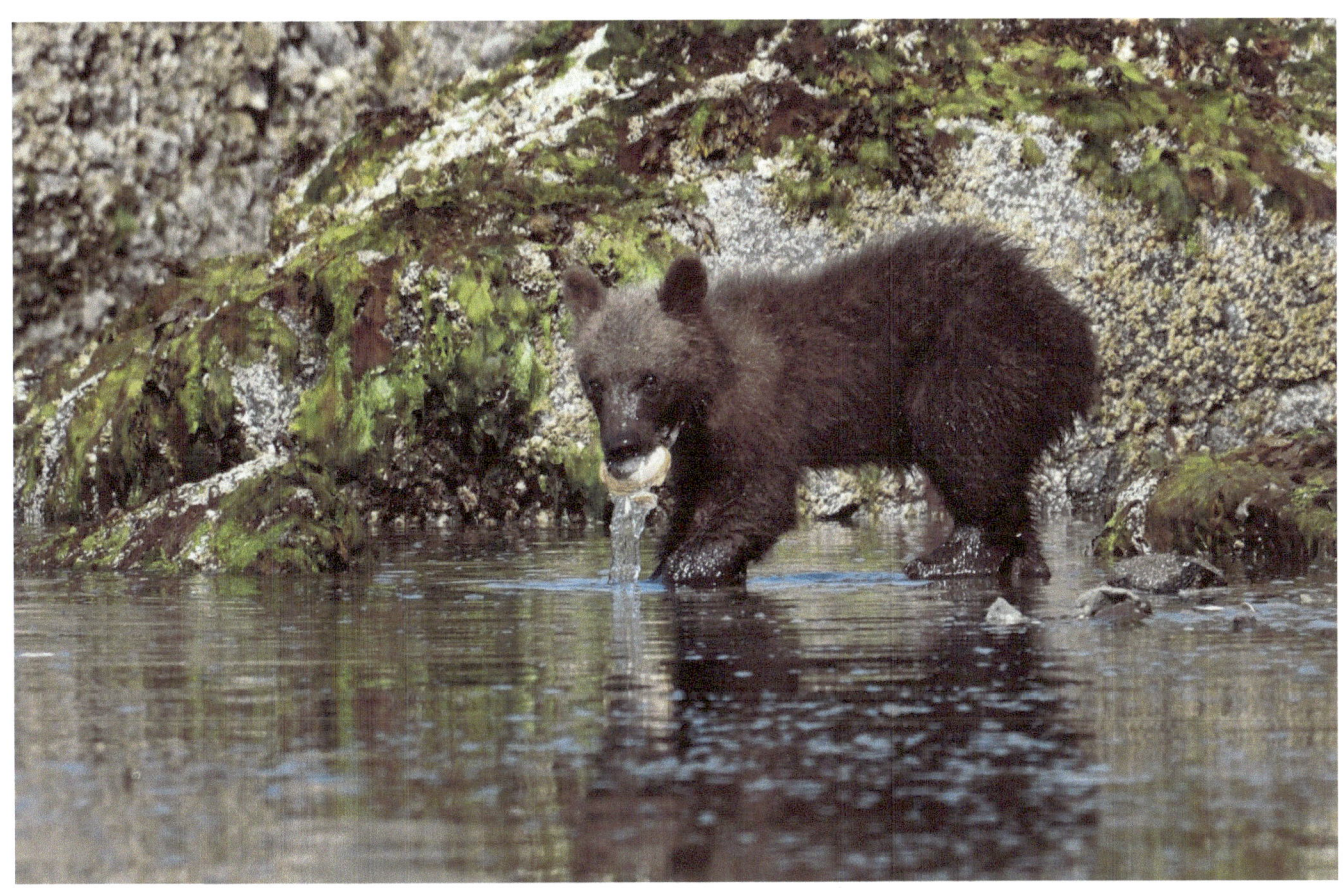

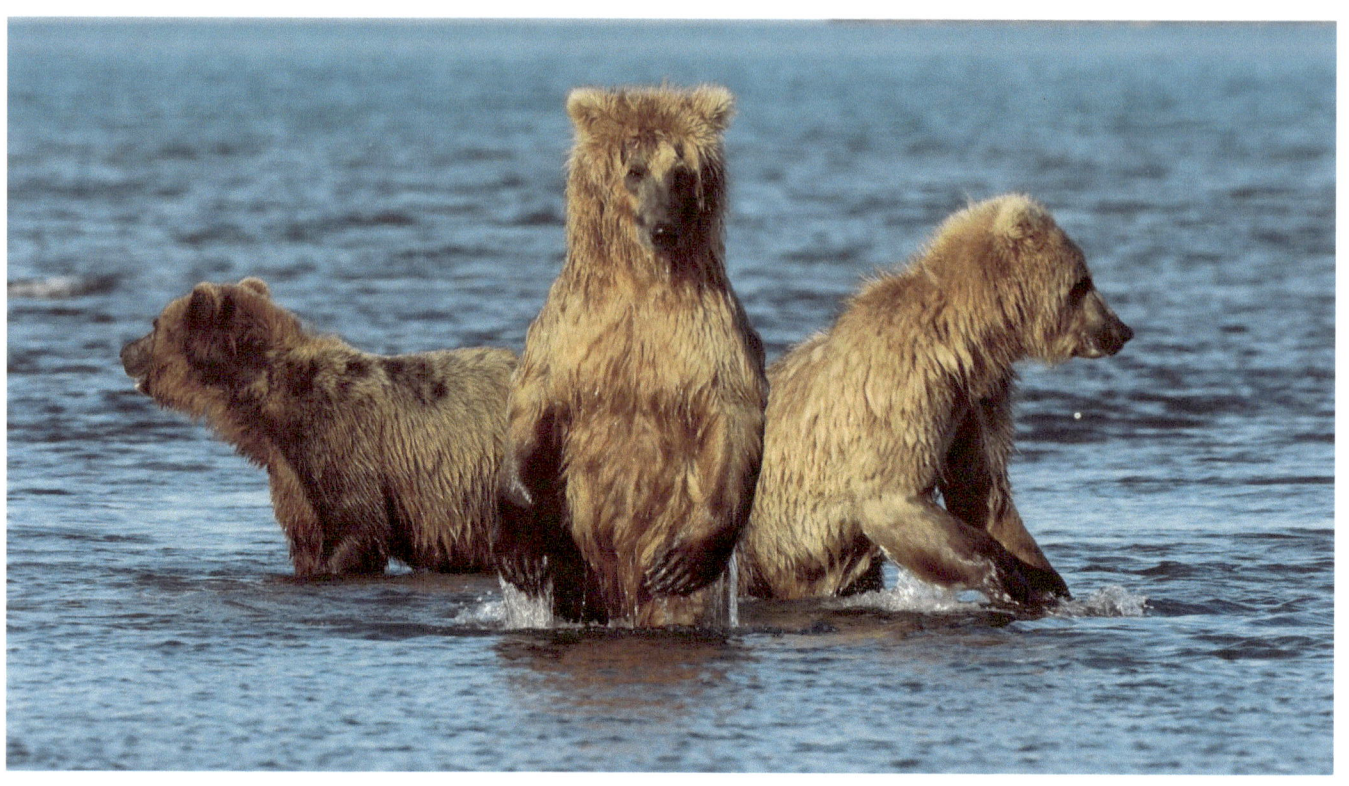

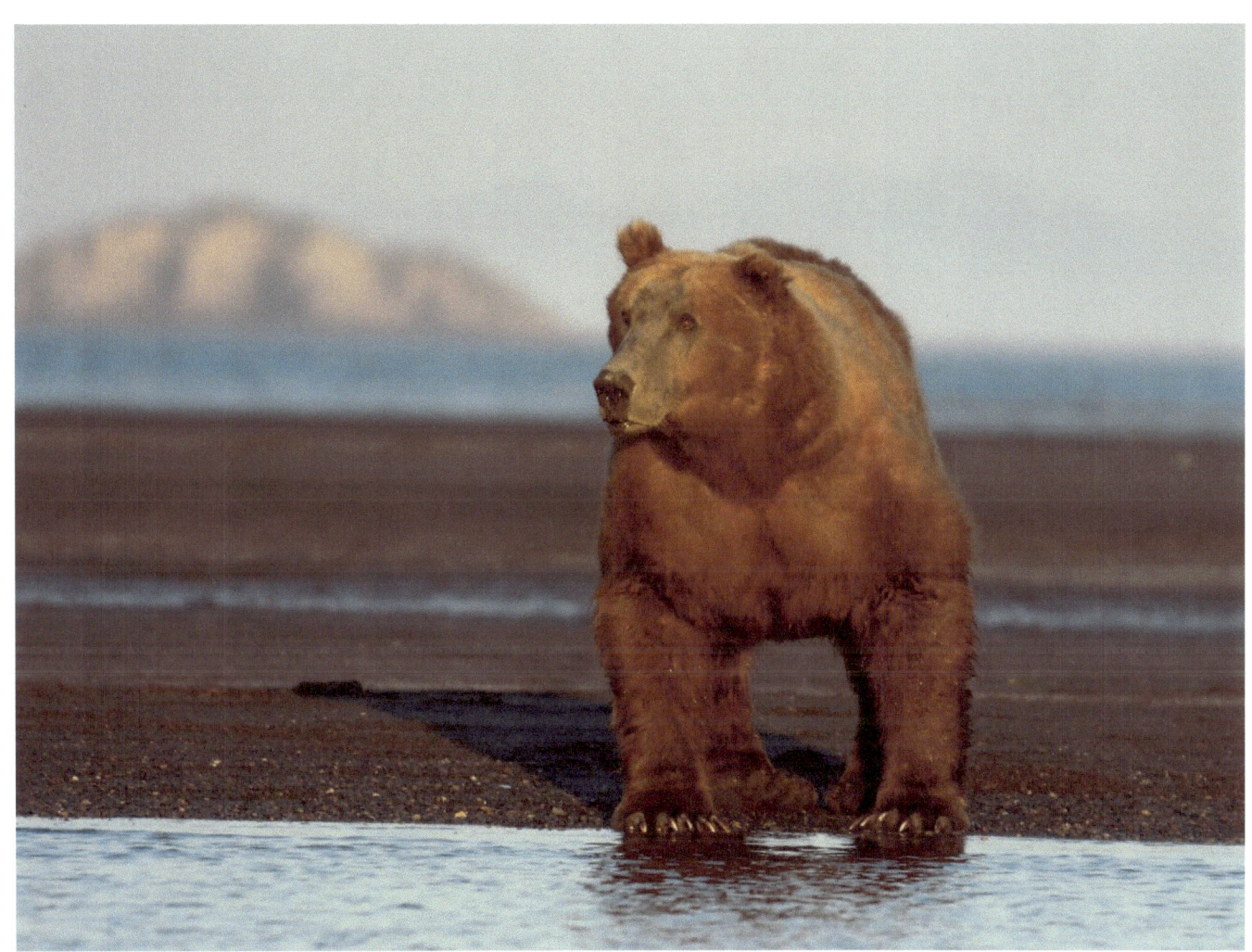

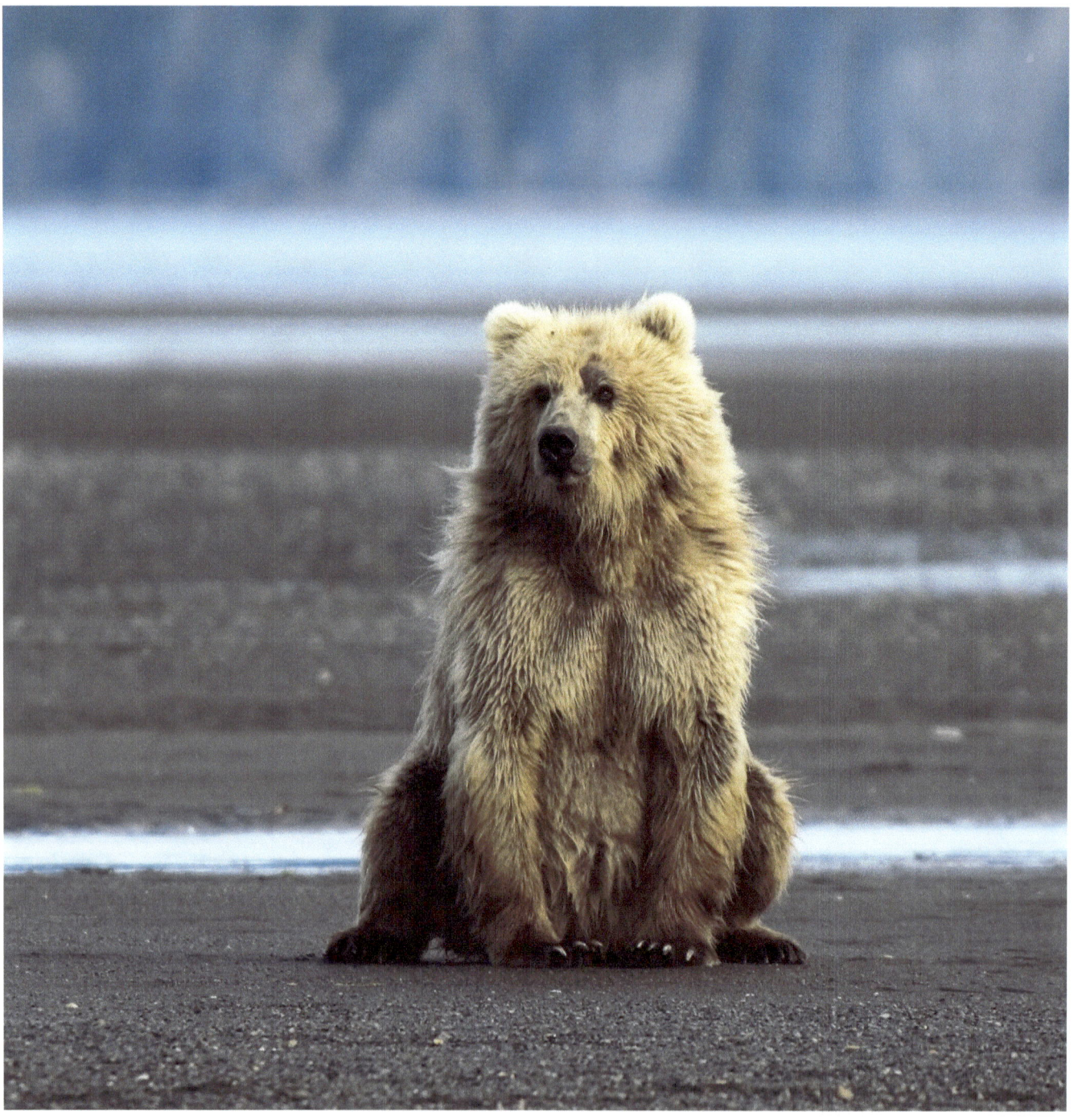

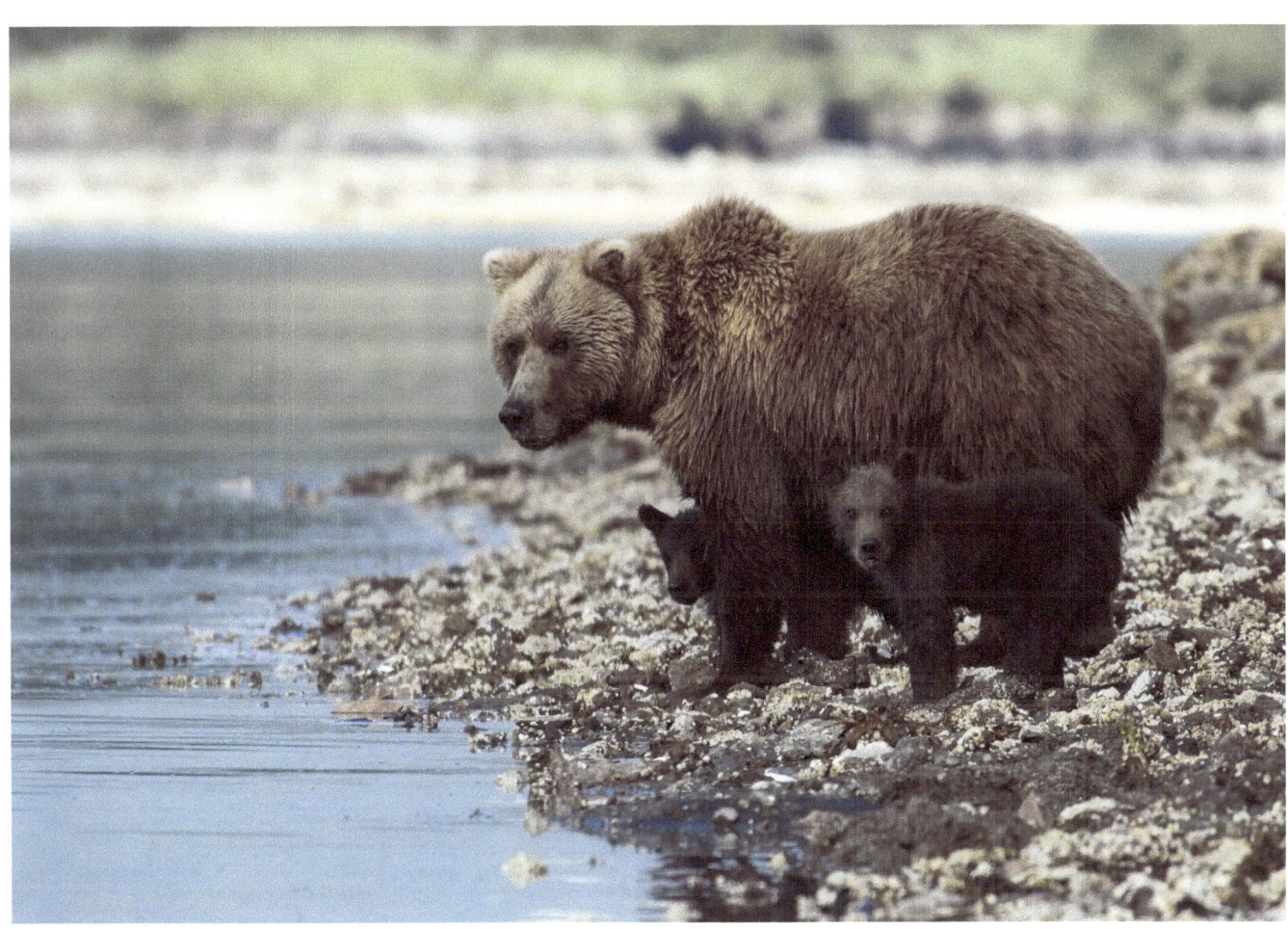

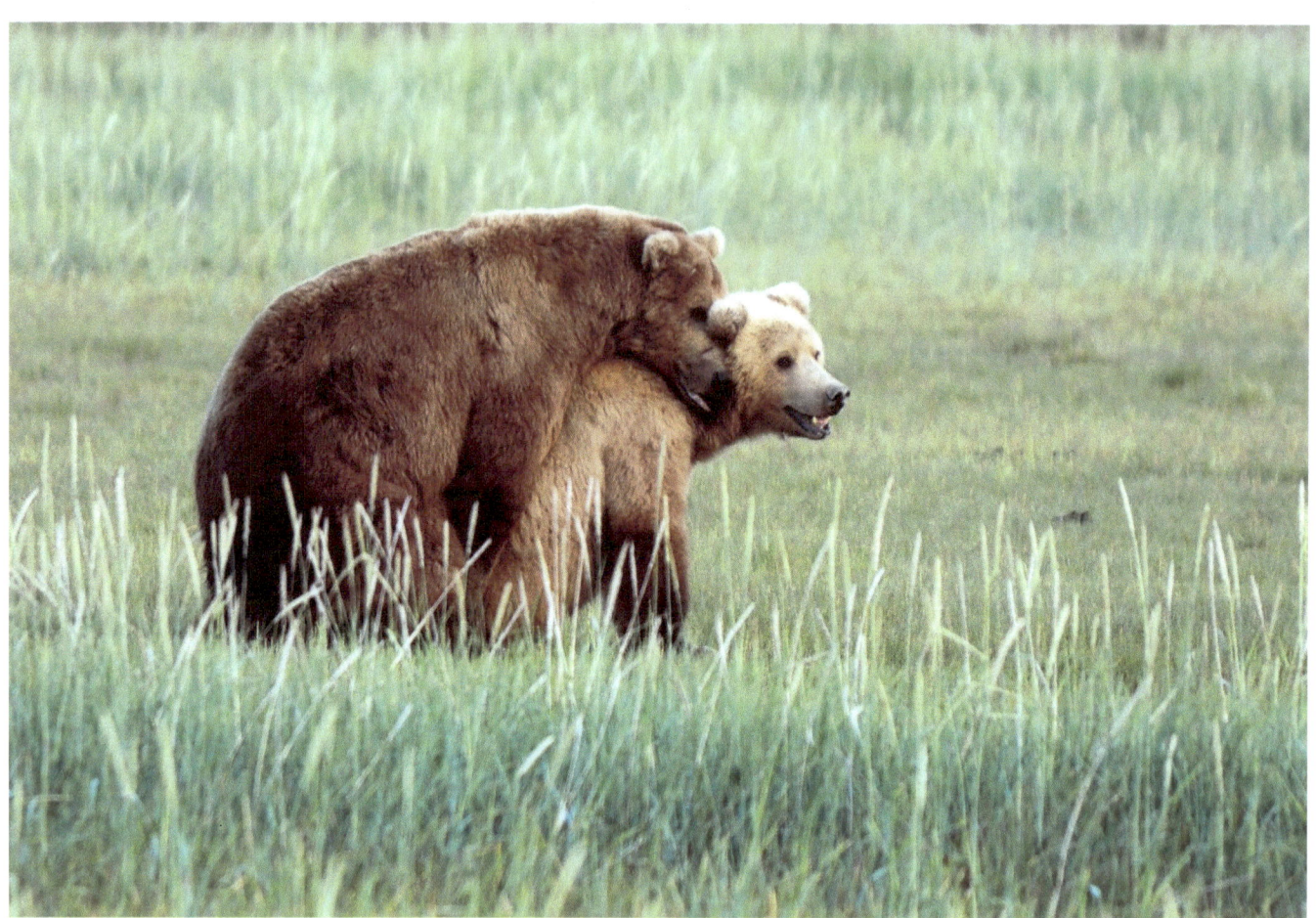

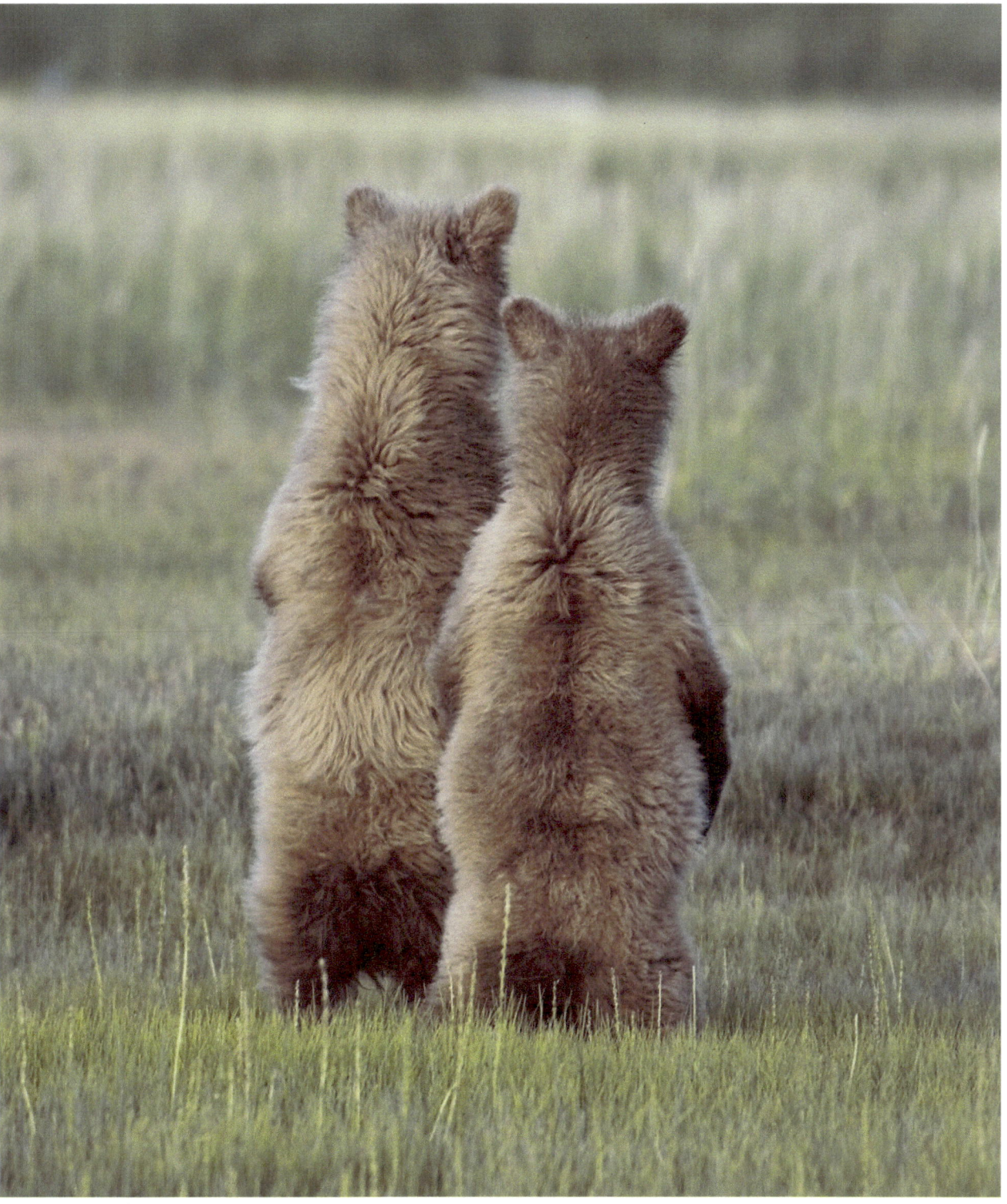

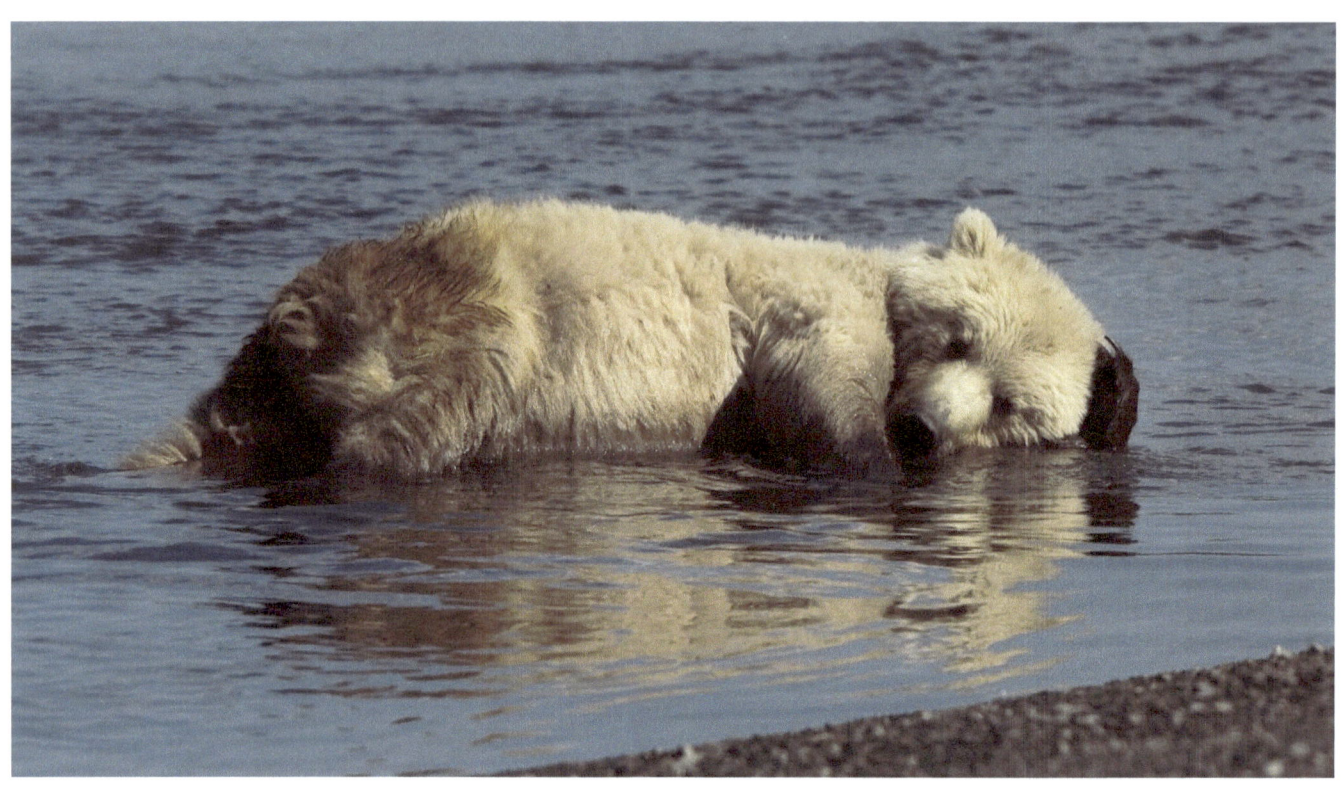

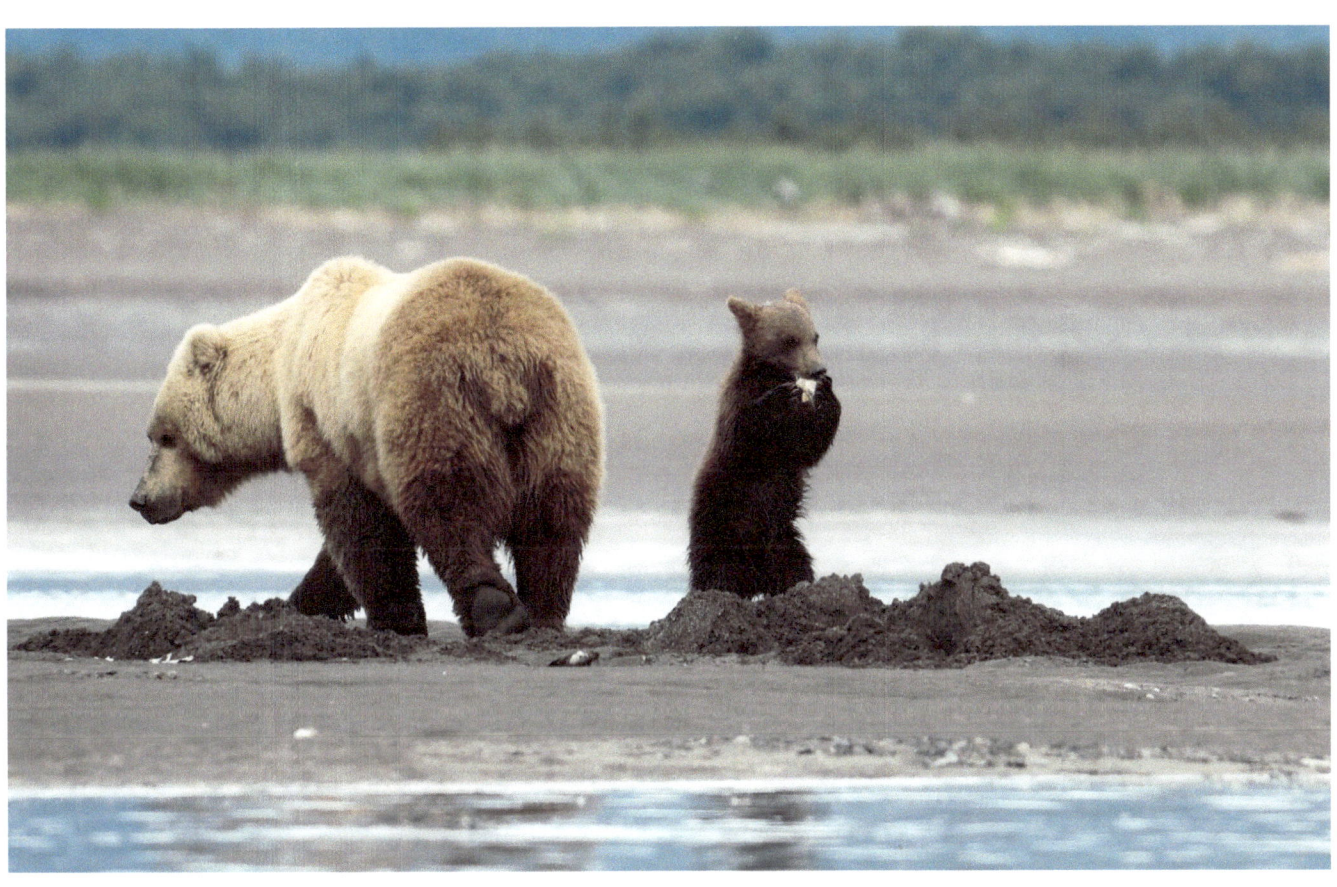

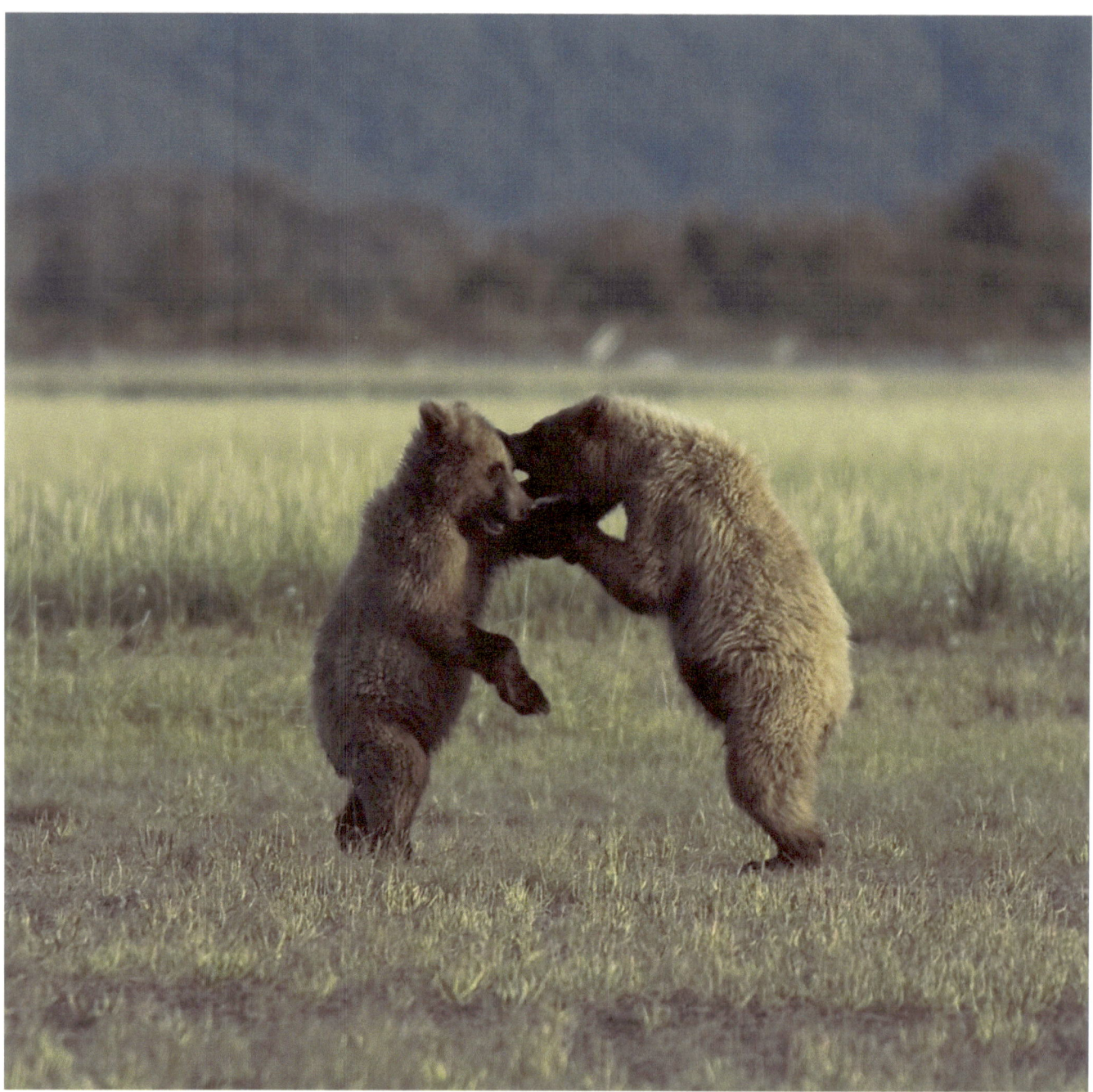

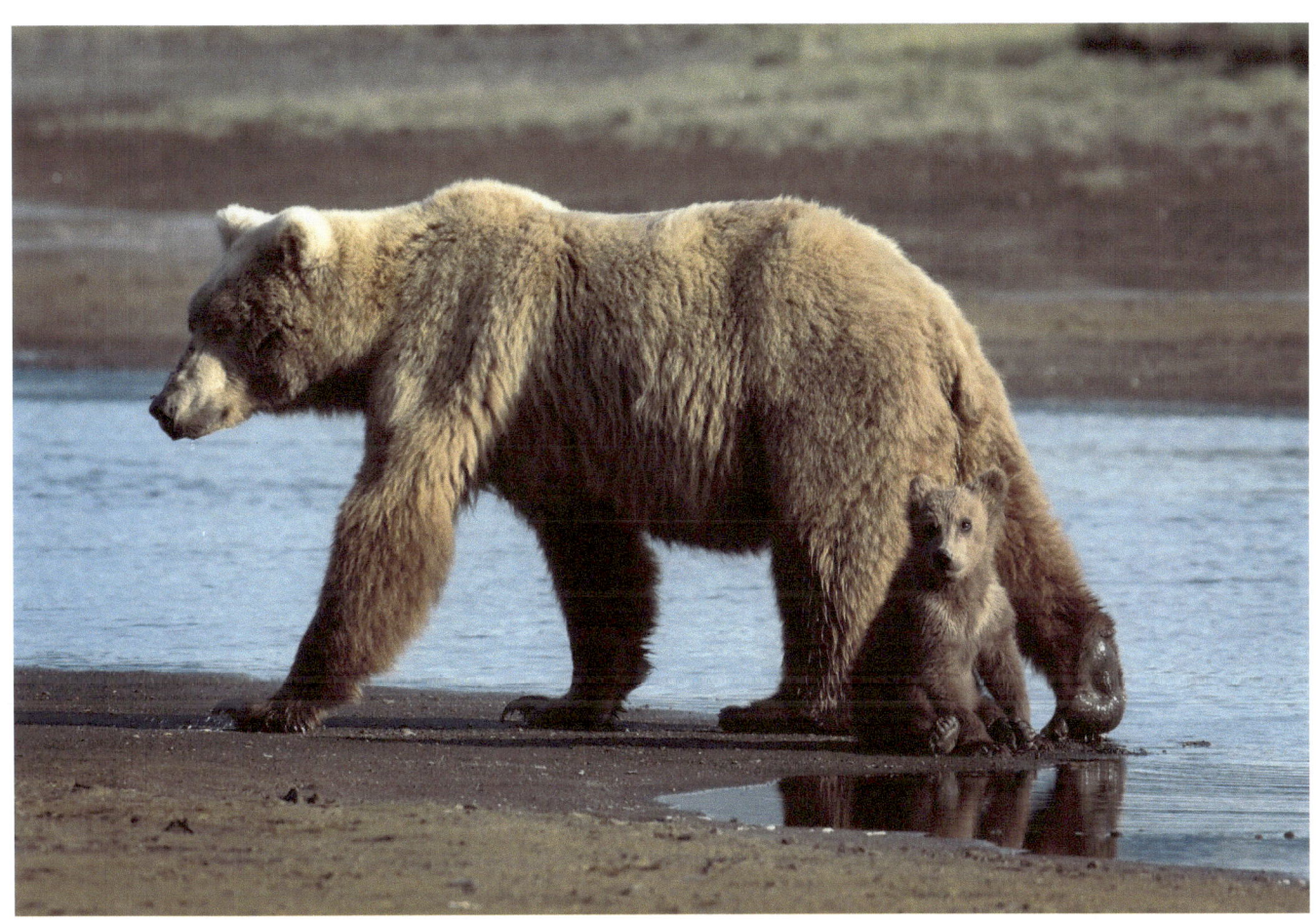

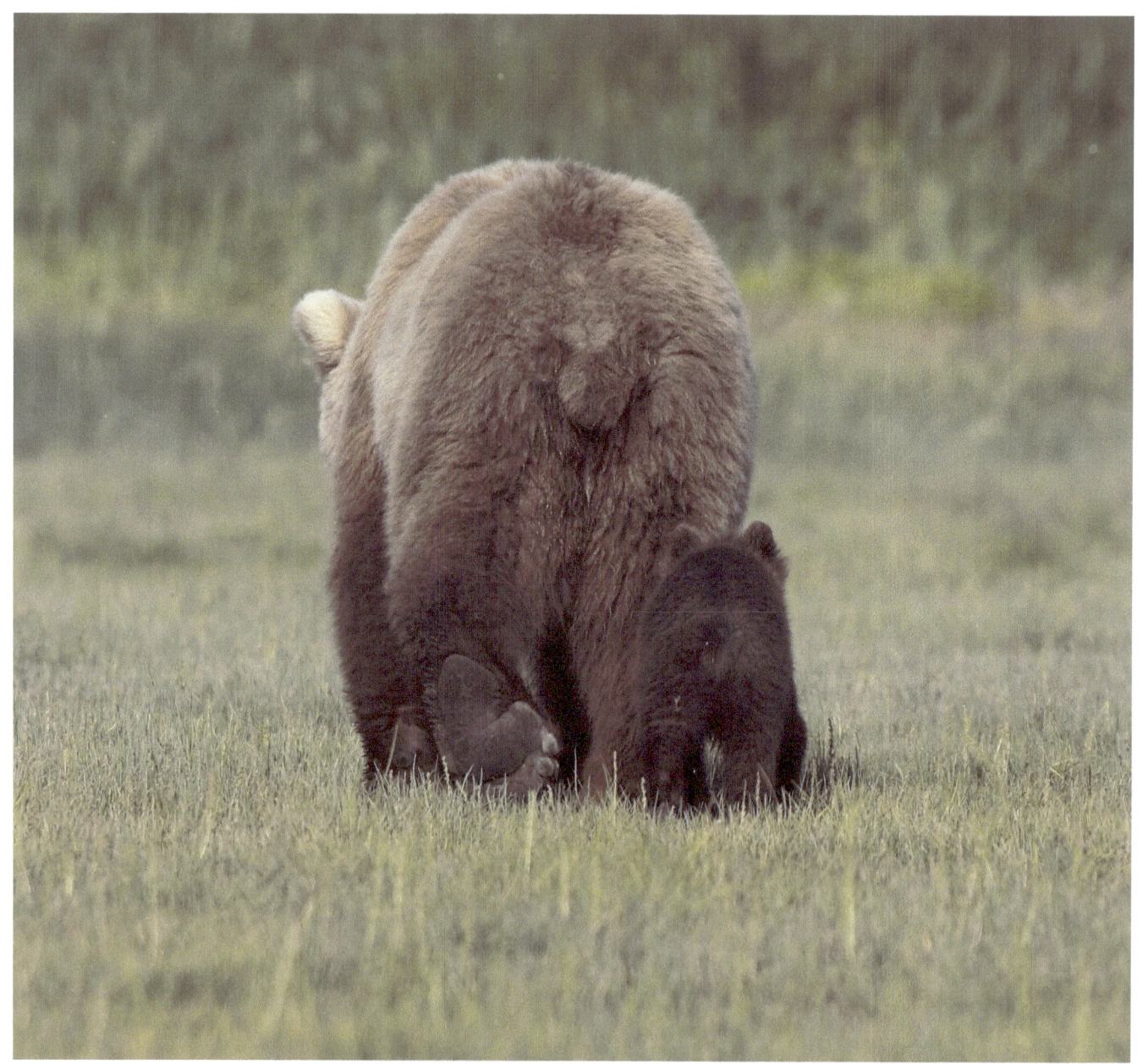

About the Photographer

Born and raised in Michigan, I spent summers at the lake, swimming, catching frogs, and chasing fireflies, winters building things out of cardboard and construction paper, writing stories, and dreaming of faraway places. Since I didn't make honors English in high school, I thought I couldn't write. So I started hanging out in the art room. The day I borrowed a camera, my love affair with photography began. Long before the birth of the pixel, I was exposing real silver halides to light and marveling at the magic of an image appearing on paper under a red light.

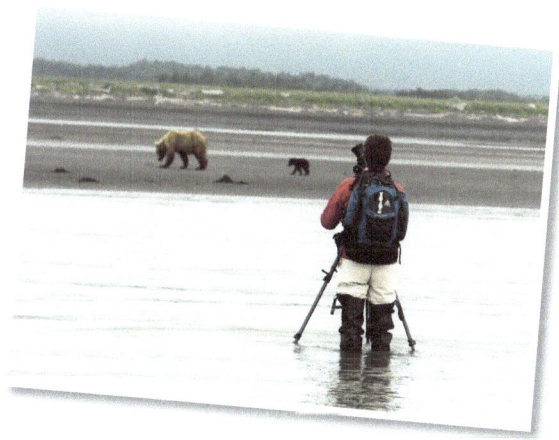

After college, I freelanced in commercial photography studios. During the long days of rigging strobes, stories skipped through my mind. As happens in life though, I was possessed by another dream—to be a wildlife photographer. I trekked through the woods to find loons, grizzly bears, whales, and moose. Then, for six years, I put my heart and soul into publishing a nature magazine, *Whisper in the Woods*. But it was not meant to be my magnum opus. This time, my attention was drawn skyward. I'd always been fascinated by the aurora borealis, shimmering in the night sky, but now my focus went beyond, to the cosmos, to wonder about our place in the universe.

In the spring of 2010, I sat down at the computer, started typing words, and breathed life into a curious boy named Kiran in *The Path to the Sun*. Together, in our quest for truth, Kiran and I have explored the mind and spirit. Our journey has taken us to places of new perspective. Alas, the answers always seem just beyond our grasp, as elusive as a firefly on a warm autumn night.

Most recently, my focus has shifted to more pressing issues—imperiled wildlife. With the Poppy McVie series, I hope to bring some light into the shadowy underworld of black market wildlife trade, where millions of wild animals are captured or slaughtered annually to fund organized crime. **IT. MUST. STOP.**

If you'd like to learn more and stay in touch, please sign up for my newsletter or follow my blog at www.KimberliBindschatel.com

www.ingramcontent.com/pod-product-compliance
Lightning Source LLC
Chambersburg PA
CBHW050757180526
45159CB00003B/1495